How To Build a 7 Figure Real Estate Team.

Unlocking Wealth: The Ultimate Guide to 7-figure Real Estate Business.

Gary S. Nichols.

Table Of Contents

Foreword…………………………… 03

Introduction…………………………..10

Part I: Laying the Foundation

Chapter 1: The Real Estate Team Blueprint …………………………20

Chapter 2.

Assembling Your Dream Team…….40

Part II: Building Your Brand

Chapter 3: Branding Your Real Estate Team…………………………..72

Chapter 4.

Leveraging Technology and Tools…100

Part III: Lead Generation and Conversion

Chapter 5: Effective Lead Generation Strategies …………………………124

Chapter 6.

Converting Leads into Clients……...154

Part IV: Scaling Your Team and Business

Chapter 7: Expanding Your Team....184

Chapter 8. Scaling Your Operations.................208
Part V: Thriving in a Competitive Market
Chapter 9: Navigating Market Challenges. 232
Chapter 10. Achieving Long-Term Success...................................262
Conclusion: Building Your Legacy in Real Estate…...............................296
About The Book 310
About The Author.......................314

Foreword.

In the dynamic field of real estate, where possibilities and obstacles always dance together, the idea that teamwork is the key to success is becoming more and more clear. The laws of success are being rewritten by real estate professionals who recognize the transforming power of teamwork. This book, "How to Build a 7-Figure Real Estate Team," is your key to unlocking that potential.

As the book's author, I've had the honor of navigating the complex real estate industry and speaking with experts whose tales have motivated me. I'm thrilled to share with you the amazing power of real estate teams, as demonstrated by their travels.

Imagine a bustling seaside community with boundless miles of immaculate beaches and exciting city life.

A real estate agent named Mark lived in the center of this utopia. Mark had a strong work ethic and extensive experience navigating the real estate market. But he found himself pushed to the breaking point as the business developed and client expectations became more complex.

One day, following another restless night spent balancing the intricacies of real estate transactions, Mark has a revelation. He understood that he needed to put together an exceptional real estate team if he was going to genuinely succeed and give his clients the kind of service they deserved.

Mark looked for people who shared his vision and who could provide new insights and complementary abilities. They worked as a powerful team, with each member lending a special expertise to the group's endeavor.

Success for the team increased as it grew. Customers were astounded by the degree of experience and the smoothness of the transactions. The team's cohesiveness and common goal yielded remarkable outcomes, turning the seven-figure milestone into a real possibility.

Mark's tale serves as evidence of the effectiveness of real estate teams. His story serves as an example of how embracing teamwork and utilizing a variety of abilities can help you grow your real estate company to new heights.

Achieving a level of balance and fulfillment that frequently eludes individuals who pursue the real estate path alone is equally important as achieving financial success.

An exploration of the core of this revolutionary idea can be found in "The Power of Real Estate Teams". It is evidence that having a real estate team on your side may propel you towards building a seven-figure business. It's about attaining financial independence and pursuing your real estate passion while working smarter, not harder.

This book provides you with a thorough examination of real estate teams that have achieved seven figures, along with insightful advice, practical tips, and insightful stories. The experiences and tales revealed within these pages will guide you, regardless of your level of experience in the real estate industry and your desire to learn from the best.

Thus, keep in mind that you are entering a world of limitless opportunities as you go out on this adventure into the real estate team industry. These narratives explore a variety of topics, including work-life balance, personal development, and the amazing potential of teamwork in addition to financial success.

Get ready to be inspired as you explore "How to Build a 7-Figure Real Estate Team" and welcome. I hope these pages serve as your road map to reaching your goals and becoming financially independent while utilizing the unmatched power of real estate teams.

Start the journey now.

Introduction

There lived a real estate agent named Sarah in the center of the busy city, where skyscrapers pierced the sky and the real estate market flowed like a river of possibilities.
Sarah was an absolute maestro in the field of real estate transactions; she was passionate about what she did. Her phone would not stop ringing since she had spent years navigating the constantly changing real estate market and earning a reputation for excellence.

However, despite her success in her career, Sarah encountered a problem that many in the real estate industry can identify with.

Real estate transactions have become increasingly complex due to the industry's exponential growth in demands. She had restless nights managing complex negotiations, a never-ending backlog of paperwork, and her clients' constantly demanding standards. She was at a crossroads in her career, which she loved. She understood that a shift in approach was necessary for her to reach the next level of achievement.

While sipping her coffee one evening, Sarah experienced a revelation. She realized that real estate teams' transformational power held the key to achieving exponential success instead of lone efforts. Sarah set out to put together the ideal group of experts who would share her enthusiasm, vision, and dedication to quality.

The combination of talent on this new team was greater than the sum of its parts. The experienced negotiator with skill at closing transactions, the marketing wizard with the ability to create eye-catching property listings, and the tech-savvy strategist familiar with the digital terrain of the contemporary real estate market. They created a formidable force in real estate together.

While there were difficulties along the way, Sarah experienced unmatched success, growth, and a work-life balance that had eluded her for a very long time. Along with opening the door to seven-figure success with her real estate business, Sarah had also discovered her freedom to enjoy life away from the office.

Real estate professionals have realized the transforming power of real estate teams, and Sarah's story is just one example among many. Along the way, she learned the tremendous value of teamwork and a diversity of skills. We explore this insight at the center of our book, "How to Build a 7-Figure Real Estate Team."

The real estate market is undergoing a significant transition, with a new generation of professionals replacing the conventional lone wolf agents. These professionals understand that collaboration is the key to achieving seven-figure success. This book is your manual for embracing teamwork, creating a winning real estate team, and attaining exceptional financial success all while preserving your love for the field.

The tales, tactics, and wisdom offered in these pages will direct your course whether you're an experienced real estate agent or a novice hoping to make seven figures. You're going to travel into the realm of real estate teams, where your goals of having a balanced work-life schedule and financial independence will come true.

This is "How to Build a 7-Figure Real Estate Team." I hope these anecdotes and encounters serve as a source of motivation, a guide, and a demonstration of the remarkable strength of real estate teams.

Why Strive for 7 Figures?

Seven has a certain aura when it comes to real estate. It's more than just a number; it's an emblem of success, a lighthouse of

hope, and proof of what's achievable. Achieving seven figures in real estate involves pursuing not only a monetary objective but also a novel lifestyle, increased autonomy, and an elevated benchmark of achievement.
Allow me to take you on a journey to demonstrate why aiming for seven digits is a transforming as well as a respectable goal.

Introducing David, a real estate agent who began his profession similar to many others. Working hard, he closed agreements and developed a consistent clientele. Although David was happy, he wanted more. He realized that making seven figures in real estate wasn't only about getting paid more. It stood for the ability to take charge of his life and mold it into the vision he had for it.

David has always had a strong desire to see the world, discover new locations, and engage with diverse cultures. But his schedule had been harsh because he was a traditional real estate agent. He had little time to appreciate the world he so greatly admired since he was so dependent on his office, phone, and clients. His passport to freedom was a seven-figure salary, and he was determined to get it.

David chose to form a real estate team in order to achieve his recently discovered objective. He assembled a group of gifted experts, each of whom contributed their special abilities and viewpoints.

This group produced an amazing synergy. His postings were seen by more people, negotiations went more smoothly, and clients received unmatched service.

David discovered that, in addition to attaining his financial objectives, his real estate team's success allowed him to recapture something even more valuable: time.

Now that a large portion of the business was being handled by his staff, he could at last travel and experience the globe he had always wanted to. He was able to manage his personal and professional lives, travel, and make memories thanks to his seven-figure salary.

David's tale serves as evidence of the transformational impact that pursuing seven figures in real estate can have. It's about more than just building wealth; it's about taking back your own time, becoming financially independent, and following your hobbies.

It's about designing a life in which you make the decisions and achieve success beyond the bounds of a conventional real estate profession.

In "How to Build a 7-Figure Real Estate Team," we explore the tactics, perceptions, and life lessons that can help you reach this important goal. It's a route that gives you the ability to create the life you've always imagined in addition to reinventing your profession.

Hence, why strive for seven digits? The solution is obvious:
Rise above the commonplace, claim your independence, and build a life rich in experiences, passions, and the satisfaction of living according to your own terms.

Let the tale of David and others like him motivate you to reach your goals, assemble your real estate team, and start your own seven-figure real estate career as you read through the upcoming chapters. You may redefine success on this journey and live the life you've always wanted.

Thank you for entering the realm of "How to Build a 7-Figure Real Estate Team." I hope it serves as your beacon of hope as you journey toward a prosperous and fulfilling life.

Part I: Laying the Foundation

Chapter 1: The Real Estate Team Blueprint

For a brief minute, picture yourself as an architect, standing at the location of a great building that is about to be built. A blueprint, or comprehensive plan that describes every facet of the building's design and construction, is essential to the project's success. The plan serves as the building block for the skyscraper, directing each stage of construction to guarantee that it realizes all of its potential.

Building a skyscraper is comparable to accomplishing the enormous accomplishment of a seven-figure salary in the real estate industry. It needs a blueprint, a carefully considered strategy that establishes the parameters for your travels. This plan is knitted into the very fabric of your real estate team, not printed on paper. It's the key to achieving your goals and the route map to your financial goals.

I'd like to present you to Samantha, a driven real estate agent who is determined to make seven figures in her career. Samantha realized that she would need assistance. To climb the success ladder, she required a guide and a group of supporters. Her experience serves as evidence of the effectiveness of the real estate team model.

In the beginning, Samantha worked
nonstop to close agreements and take care
of her clients as a lone agent.
Although she saw benefits from her
efforts, she was aware that she would not
be able to achieve her goal of a
seven-figure salary without making a
tactical change. She started by
meticulously creating her blueprint for a
real estate team.

Samantha's vision and objectives served as
the cornerstone of her plan. She had an
image of a group of experts who were as
driven to succeed as she was and who
shared her commitment to quality. She
went out to locate the ideal people to join
her mission with certain goals in mind.

Samantha placed a strong emphasis on
skill diversity as she grew her staff. She

brought in specialists in technology, client relations, marketing, and negotiating, among other areas of real estate. Samantha's business flourished due to the exceptional synergy formed by her diversified skill set.

Beyond only abilities, Samantha's real estate team model included a common culture of excellence and customer-focused service. Every client enjoyed the greatest experience possible because of the team's persistent devotion to these principles.

With her plan in place, Samantha's business took off. She discovered that she was completing deals faster, serving clients more skillfully, and hitting financial milestones that she had only ever dreamed of. Her life and her career had changed as a result of her real estate team's success.

The tale of Samantha and her real estate group serves as a striking example of the influence of a meticulously designed blueprint. In "How to Build a 7-Figure Real Estate Team," we'll go into the tactics and perspectives that will assist you in establishing the groundwork necessary to reach seven figures.

Your real estate team's plan is as important for accomplishing new heights of success as a construction blueprint is for building a skyscraper.
Thus, keep Samantha's tale in mind as you go through the upcoming chapters and how your real estate team blueprint can change lives. It's more than simply a plan; it's your route to achieve your desired

lifestyle, career fulfillment, and financial freedom.

Thank you for entering the realm of "How to Build a 7-Figure Real Estate Team." You have the blueprint to your own success.
In addition, many people in the real estate industry find it intriguing to strive for a seven-figure income.

Although achieving such financial achievement is not easy, it is possible to travel with strategy and accuracy. Your road map is this book,
"How to Build a 7-Figure Real Estate Team," and the foundation of your journey is the Real Estate Team Blueprint.

The blueprint is essentially a strategy plan that describes your real estate team's organization, responsibilities, and procedures. It serves as both the cornerstone for your company and your path to financial success. You must realize the importance of this blueprint when you enter the world of highly compensated real estate agents.

A clear vision is the first step in creating your real estate team blueprint. You need to outline your objectives, your ideal income, and the strategy you plan to use to get there. Your real estate team's actions and decisions are inspired and guided by this vision, which acts as a beacon.

You'll list each team member's duties and responsibilities in your blueprint. This means that a cohesive and effective team must be assembled by carefully choosing people whose talents complement one another. Whether it's technology, client relations, marketing, or negotiating, the variety of skills on your team is essential to your success.

Another essential element of your plan is culture. Your team will be defined by its common principles, work ethics, and client-centered approach. What will make you stand out in the business is your team's unwavering focus to delivering outstanding service and their passion to perfection.

Your real estate team will function with unprecedented efficiency and coherence as you adhere to the blueprint. You will be able to close more business, provide better customer service, and make more money. The plan turns into the engine that propels your financial and professional development.

We will go deeper into the tactics, perspectives, and best practices needed to create your real estate team blueprint and make the transition to a seven-figure income in the upcoming chapters of this book. It's a thorough manual created to provide you the skills and information needed to establish a successful real estate team.

Your blueprint is more than simply a plan; it serves as the cornerstone of your goals and the driving force behind your success in the future. You're well on your way to becoming a seven-figure real estate team with a solid blueprint in place. Welcome to the exciting world of "How to Build a 7-Figure Real Estate Team," where the

Real Estate Team Blueprint is the first step on your path to both professional and financial success.

Outlining Your Objectives and Vision.

Success in the real estate industry is frequently quantified in terms of numbers and figures. The desire to earn the coveted seven-figure salary is a motivating factor for many people. But getting to this level of financial success starts with a crucial—and sometimes missed—step: figuring out what your objectives and vision are.

Your route to a seven-figure real estate team will be constructed around your goals and ambitions. They provide your actions and decisions direction, inspiration, and meaning. Now, let's begin the vital step of defining your objectives

and creating a plan for your real estate
endeavors.

The Influence of Sense.

To start, your best ally is clarity. Be
precise and thorough in describing your
objectives. Rather than just aiming for a
"high income," make a specific financial
goal. "What does a seven-figure income
mean to me?" is a question to consider. Is
it the capacity to invest in specific
projects, a particular lifestyle, or a set
quantity of yearly earnings? Making a plan
to accomplish your goal is easier the more
specific it is.

Both short- and long-term objectives.,
You should have both short- and long-term
goals in mind. A few examples of
short-term objectives are quarterly sales
targets, client acquisition objectives, or

mastery of a new marketing tactic. On the other side, long-term objectives can include growing your real estate company into new areas or hitting your seven-figure income target within the following several years.

Formulating an Idea.

Creating a vision for your real estate journey is just as vital as achieving your goals. The main idea that motivates your aspirations is called your vision. It describes the kind of real estate agent you hope to become and the kind of legacy you hope to leave. Your actions are shaped and your enthusiasm is fueled by a captivating vision.

Illustration.

By practicing visualization, you can bring your vision to life. Picture yourself leading a prosperous real estate team in the future. Imagine the way of life, the achievements, and the difference you want to create. On difficult days, this mental image can serve as a strong source of inspiration and motivation.

Compliance with Individual Principles., Your personal values should be in line with your aims and vision. This connection guarantees that your quest for achievement will be purposeful and gratifying. Your objectives ought to demonstrate your dedication to truthful and moral real estate procedures, for instance, if integrity is important to you.

Flexibility.

Finally, as your trip develops, be ready to modify your objectives and vision. The real estate market is ever-changing, so things could change for you. When you choose an adaptive strategy, you can stay on course and modify your goals to take advantage of new possibilities or overcome obstacles.

As you set out on the path described in "How to Build a 7-Figure Real Estate Team," keep in mind that creating your vision and goals is an ongoing process. It's a continuous process that needs to develop together with you. You are prepared to construct a successful seven-figure real estate team if your goals provide a clear roadmap and your vision is engaging. So, aim high and let your objectives and vision serve as a compass to guide you toward your achievement in both your career and finances.

The Seven-Figure Team Anatomy

Creating a seven-figure real estate team is an accomplishment that calls for a meticulous plan, steadfast dedication, and a thorough comprehension of the fundamental components that hold everything together. Similar to building an impressive edifice, a seven-figure real estate team requires meticulous preparation and a strong basis. We are going to go into the blueprint that outlines the fundamental structure of a team that achieves such high standards in "How to Build a 7-Figure Real Estate Team."

1. Leadership Quality: The Foundation

Every profitable seven-figure real estate team is built around a leader who possesses a certain set of abilities. The cornerstone of the foundation of your team is excellence in leadership. As the ship's captain, you have to demonstrate the capacity to motivate, lead, and direct your group toward a single objective. Reputable leadership cultivates a climate of growth, accountability, and trust.

2. Hiring and Acquiring Talent:
You need talented people on your team if you want to establish a 7-figure operation. Having the appropriate people in the right places is ensured by careful recruitment and talent acquisition. Having a methodical approach to hiring and a sharp eye for talent helps position your team for success.

3. Goal-setting and Strategic Planning:
Planning strategically is the key to your success. Your goals serve as road signs as your team follows this plan toward a vision. Among other important elements,

your strategic plan should cover lead generation, marketing methods, expansion plans, and client relations.

4. Effective Procedures and Systems:

Effectiveness is the key in the real estate industry. Systems and procedures that are effective must be in place within your team to manage everything from property transactions to customer onboarding. Not only does streamlining these procedures save time, but it also improves the client experience in general.

5. Sturdy Promotion and Lead Creation:

In a cutthroat real estate market, lead creation and marketing are essential to your success. You may guarantee a consistent stream of customers and referrals by using social media, developing a strong offline and online presence, and creating a network of contacts.

6. Management Of Client Relationships:

Superior customer relationship management is the foundation of a seven-figure organization. Establishing credibility, being aware of your clients' demands, and offering flawless service are essential to your success.

7. Investment and Financial Management:

To make seven figures, you need to be an expert in money management. This entails prudent financial decision-making, growth investment, and astute budgeting.

8. Education and Training:

Your team members' ongoing education and training will keep them at the forefront of the field. Empowering your staff with the newest tools and industry trends is a strategic advantage since knowledge truly is power.

9. Flexibility and Creativity:

The real estate market is always changing. Seven-figure teams that are successful are able to innovate in response to fresh opportunities and challenges as well as adjust to changes in the market.

10. Zeal And Tenacity:

Ultimately, the intangible components that keep your team driven and unwavering in their quest for achievement are passion and resilience. What distinguishes 7-figure teams is a fierce drive to succeed along with an unwavering attitude in the face of difficulty.

As you read through "How to Build a 7-Figure Real Estate Team," remember that these ten elements are the foundation of your team's success plan. Reaching the coveted 7-figure milestone requires the harmonious operation of all interrelated elements. Thus, get ready to go out on a path that will revolutionize your real estate pursuits and bring you to the highest level of professional success.

Chapter 2.

Assembling Your Dream Team

Imagine this: An experienced realtor, let's refer to her as Staring at her ambitious business strategy, Sarah sits in her office. She sees a prosperous seven-figure real estate team that is unmatched in all facets. She is conscious of one important reality, though: she cannot fulfill her desire by herself.

Every prosperous seven-figure real estate team is a collaborative work of art, a patchwork of special abilities, dispositions, and talents that come together to make a cohesive and productive whole. Sarah saw the value of putting together the ideal team she had always imagined as she set out to create one.

The Basis of Achievement.

Sarah came to understand that a successful real estate team is built on its individuals. They are the lifeblood of the organization, and each member's performance elevates the group as a whole. It's similar to making a gorgeous mosaic; every component is necessary, and when put together skillfully, they create a work of art.

Finding the Correct Components.

Sarah started her trip by choosing the appropriate mosaic pieces. She was aware that she would require a varied team, with each member contributing a special set of abilities and capabilities. She didn't simply want the finest salesmen on her ideal team—she also wanted the best team. She conducted interviews, went to real estate events, and combed through her network. The objective was to locate people that shared her vision, values, and work ethic in addition to having the requisite real estate experience. She understood that it was more crucial to find the correct fit than to just fill jobs.

Boosting Personality.

After gathering her team, Sarah realized how critical it was to value each person's uniqueness. As every fragment in a mosaic possesses a particular color and shape, so too did each team member contribute their own strengths to the collective. Regardless of their specialty—marketing, negotiating, client relations, or administrative support—Sarah urged all team members to excel in it.

Assembling a Whole in Harmony. Sarah also realized that a mosaic is a skillfully constructed arrangement rather than just a chance gathering of fragments. She led her team toward a shared vision and objective, acting as the glue that kept them all together. She created a team-oriented atmosphere where assistance and communication were crucial. Sarah made sure that everyone on her team worked together, much like a conductor directing an orchestra.

The Mosaic's Beautiful Design. Sarah witnessed her ambition realized as her seven-figure real estate team prospered. Not only was the mosaic she had put together a representation of her accomplishment, but it also demonstrated the strength of teamwork. The team's varied personalities, abilities, and skills came together to form a cohesive, high-performing unit that continuously produced excellent outcomes.

In "How to Build a 7-Figure Real Estate Team," we'll go into the nuances of putting together your ideal group of people, fostering their unique talents, and becoming a cohesive unit. You'll find that you too can create a real estate behemoth that's more than the sum of its parts, just like Sarah did. So get ready to be motivated, helped, and inspired to use the skill of putting together your ideal team to build your own masterpiece of real estate success.

Putting Together Your Dream Team: The Foundation of Excellence in Real Estate

Building a seven-figure team in the real estate business is not just a financial objective; it's a testimonial to the heights one can reach in the field. It stands for the ultimate level of achievement that many real estate agents aspire to. But it's not a voyage that can be taken by one person. You need to put together the ideal team that will be the cornerstone of your success if you want to develop a seven-figure real estate team.

The Strength of Cooperation. Constructing a seven-figure real estate team is comparable to building a skyscraper. It needs a strong base, a success plan, and a group of competent people who collaborate well. Every member of your team adds special talents and qualities to the group effort, making them each an essential component of the puzzle.

Variety and Proficiency.
A mosaic of varied skills and domains of knowledge should make up your ideal team. Having the greatest team is more important than simply having the best salesmen. Every team member should be excellent in their specific function, whether it be marketing, negotiating, customer interactions, or administrative assistance. A real estate team resembles a symphony, in which every instrument contributes uniquely to the harmonizing whole.

Similar Goals and Principles.

Ensuring that all team members align with your vision and beliefs is crucial for you as the team leader. Your ideal team should share your objectives and be dedicated to reaching them. The team moves forward when there is a sense of purpose and direction created by everyone working toward the same goal.

Boosting Personality.

As much as a strong team has a similar objective, individualism must also be valued and encouraged. Every team member contributes their special strengths to the group. Accepting these unique skills enables your team to take on a wider range of chances and challenges.

Effective Guidance.
As the leader, you play a crucial role as the glue that keeps the team together. You lead by example, establish standards, and make sure there is harmony among team members. To foster a collaborative and productive atmosphere, effective leadership, support, and communication are crucial.

The Seven-Figure Dream Came True. You will be well on your way to reaching your seven-figure real estate objectives once you've put together your ideal team. In the same way as every mosaic piece enhances the beauty of the entire piece, every team member is essential to attaining success in your real estate ventures.

We will go into more detail about the nuances of putting together your ideal team in "How to Build a 7-Figure Real Estate Team." We'll look at the tactics, guidelines, and discoveries that can help you build a dominant real estate company. You will learn the secrets to building your dream team and reaching your seven-figure goals with this book.

Positions and Accountabilities Responsibilities and Roles: The Cornerstones of a Successful Team.

Building a seven-figure team is not a solo endeavor in the sphere or realm of real estate. It's therefore a team effort that needs to be carefully planned, carried out, and assigned tasks, duties and responsibilities that are well defined. Your team's ability to succeed in the sphere of real estate depends on how well each member applies their special talents and carries out their assigned responsibilities.

The essential idea of roles and responsibilities is examined in this chapter using the framework of "How to Build a 7-Figure Real Estate Team."

The Dynamic Team.

Consider your team for the real estate sphere as a well-oiled machine, with every part essential to its efficient functioning. Similar to how a machine's cogs and gears mesh to accomplish a certain task, your team members should operate in unison to accomplish your shared goal. There are several elements to the real estate industry, ranging from administration and negotiating to marketing and client interactions. Every one of these aspects calls for certain people with specific roles and abilities.

Important Roles in Your Team.

1. Sales Specialists:

Your real estate transactions are powered by these individuals. They generate leads, seal sales, and make sure the sales process is efficient. When it comes to connecting with clients and helping them throughout their real estate journey, sales experts are frequently the face of your organization.

2. Marketing Experts:

Your team needs people who can strategically market your properties and brand in an era where digital platforms and marketing channels rule the day. Marketing specialists are in charge of developing and carrying out marketing strategies, preserving your web presence, and making sure that your listings get the most exposure possible.

3. Managers of Client Relationships:

These experts are committed to helping you build trusting relationships with your clients. Their duties include giving your clients outstanding service, staying in touch, and responding to any queries or problems they might have. A happy customer is frequently the source of referrals and recurring business.

4. Support for Administration:

Administrative personnel are the foundation of any successful team; they make sure everything runs smoothly. They take care of appointments, paperwork, and logistics so that other team members can concentrate on their primary duties.

5. Bargainers: Negotiators with skill are crucial in the often complicated business of real estate. They deal with contract terms, price negotiations, and making sure your clients get the best possible offer.

Lucidity and Dialogue.

Effective communication and clarity are essential for the roles and responsibilities in your team to function well. Each member of the team should be fully aware of their responsibilities and how they contribute to the success of the group as a whole. Team members must also collaborate and communicate on a regular basis. Regular team meetings, updates, and information exchange should occur.

Adaptability and Flexibility.

As important as roles and responsibilities are, it's also critical to maintain flexibility. Since the real estate market is so dynamic, things can change quickly. When it comes to taking advantage of unanticipated opportunities or difficulties, your team members should be ready to move beyond their assigned responsibilities.

Encouraging Your Team One of the most important aspects of leadership is encouraging your team to take initiative and thrive in their jobs. It promotes accountability and propels both individual and group achievement.

We explore role and responsibility in further detail in "How to Build a 7-Figure Real Estate Team." We look at how to establish your team to be as successful and efficient as possible. Gaining insight into and putting these fundamentals into practice can help you create a real estate team that can accomplish the amazing feat of seven figures.

Choosing the Correct Group Members Selecting The Proper Team Members: The Key to Success

Putting together the correct team is one of the most important elements in the process of bringing together or developing a seven-figure team in real estate. Since individual members of the team contribute to its strength, it is critical to select the best candidate for each position. The skill of choosing the correct team members is covered in this chapter of "How to Build a 7-Figure Real Estate Team." This is a process that can make or break your route to success.

The Significance of a Good Fit.
Putting together a championship sports team is similar to building a successful real estate team. Each player ought to be

selected based on how well they fit the squad as a whole, in addition to the talents and skill set of individual members. Your real estate team needs players who can thrive in their specific roles, much like a basketball team needs players who can shoot, defend, and create plays.

The Spectrum of Skill Sets.
It's critical to understand the variety of abilities and character types your team requires while selecting team members. Despite the fact that every team in real estate possess different abilities, the following common skill sets and characteristics should be adhered to or taken into consideration:

1. Experience:
In the real estate sector, experience is priceless. Seek out team members who

have demonstrated success in their
particular jobs.

2. Drive:

Ambition and tenacity are frequently
defining characteristics of successful real
estate professionals. Look for those who
are driven to go above and beyond for
clients and the success of the team.

3. Adaptability:

The industry is a dynamic one. It is
essential for team members to be able to
adjust to changing client demands and
market conditions.

4. Communication Skills:

The secret to a successful real estate deal
is effective communication. Members of
your team should be able to listen intently

to the demands of clients and clearly communicate difficult information.

5. Team Player:

While achieving individual success is important, your team should be made up of people who get along well with one another and encourage one another to work hard.

Techniques for Hiring.

To select the best team members, one must use a calculated approach:

Selecting the Proper Team Members: The Key to Success

Putting together the correct team is one of the most important elements in the process of organizing or developing a seven-figure team in real estate business. Since each/individual member in your team contributes to its strength, it is critical to select the best candidate for each position.

The skill of choosing the correct team members is covered in this chapter of "How to Build a 7-Figure Real Estate Team." This is a process that can make or break your route to success.

The Significance of a Good Fit. Putting together a championship sports club or team is synonymous to building and developing a successful team in real estate. Each player ought to be selected based on how well they fit the squad as a whole, in addition to their set of skills. The team needs players who can thrive in their specific roles, much like a basketball team needs players who can shoot, defend, and create plays.

The Spectrum of Skill Sets.
It's critical to understand the variety of abilities and character types your team requires while selecting team members. Despite the fact that there are differences in real estate teams, the following common skill sets and characteristics should be taken into account:

1. Experience:
In the real estate sector, experience is priceless. Seek out team members who

have demonstrated success in their particular jobs.

2. Drive:

Ambition and tenacity are frequently defining characteristics of successful and excelling real estate experts and professionals. Look for those who are driven to go above and beyond for their clients and for the team's success.

3. Adaptability:

The industry is a dynamic one. It is essential for members of the team to be able to adjust to changing client demands and market conditions.

4. Communication Skills:

The secret to a successful real estate deal is effective communication. Your team members should be able to listen intently to the demands of clients and clearly communicate difficult information.

5. Team Player:

While achieving individual success is important, your team should be made up of people who get along well with one another and encourage one another to work hard.

Techniques for Hiring

To select the best team members, one must use a calculated approach:

1. Networking:

Make use of the contacts you already have in the industry and your professional network. Online forums, seminars, and real estate events can be great resources for finding possible team members.

2. Posting of Jobs:

Write thorough job postings that expressly describe the responsibilities and expectations. To connect with possible applicants, use websites, employment forums for real estate, and LinkedIn.

3. Interview Procedure:

To guarantee a good match within the team, create a thorough interview procedure that includes situational questions, technical assessments, and compatibility assessments.

4. Citations:

Get references and look them over carefully to verify a candidate's claims and learn more about their prior work.

Assessing Possible and Positive Colleagues.

It's critical to evaluate prospective team members in light of your team's needs and requirements also including your long-term goals during the hiring process. Assessing how a candidate fits or adapt into the cultural fit of your team is just as crucial as evaluating their ability and experience. Effective team chemistry can make a big difference in your success.

The Path to Achievement.

We go more into the nuances of choosing the ideal individuals in a team that is focused on "How to Build a 7-Figure Real Estate Team." We give you the resources to pinpoint the people who will improve team performance and assist you in reaching your aspirational financial targets. Recall that having the correct team

members is essential to your success as
you proceed on your trip.

Culture and Team Values.
Values and Team Culture: Creating the Foundation for Success

It's simple to underestimate the significance of team ideals and culture in the industry, when deals are sometimes seen as purely financial ventures. A 7-figure real estate team may be propelled by a well-designed team culture, every seasoned real estate agent is aware of this. In this section of this book, we explore the importance and value of developing a strong team values and culture and how doing so can result in remarkable accomplishments.

How to Define Team Culture.
The collective identity, values, and customs of your team are embodied in your team's culture. It serves as the unseen adhesive holding your team together and encouraging cooperation among them as they work together to achieve a common objective. Your team's output, performance, and client satisfaction may all be fueled by a good team culture.

The Value of Team Principles.
Values serve as your team's moral compass. They serve as a guide for team decision-making, morality, and conduct. Developing your team's culture requires that you recognize and prioritize these ideals. Integrity, openness, client-centeredness, and any other norm that are important to you in your business can be included in your values list.

The Advantages of a Positive Work Environment.

1. Increased Productivity:
A cohesive and encouraging team environment can increase output. Team members are more inclined to go above and above when they are driven and feel appreciated.

2. Better Customer Service:
A happy workplace environment that places a high priority on customer-focused principles can enhance customer satisfaction, which frequently generates more recommendations and repeat business.

3. Conflict Resolution:
Efficient conflict resolution can be facilitated by a positive team culture.

Members of a team that value and trust one another are better able to resolve conflicts in a positive path.

4. Baiting and Retaining Talents:

Prospective members of the team will always find a positive culture in the team, to be appealing. It can also be extremely important in keeping talented workers who value the workplace.

Developing the Correct Culture and Values for Your Team.

1. Set an Example:

As the team's leader, your deeds and mannerisms influence the group as a whole. Others will be motivated to adopt the same ideals by your unwavering commitment to them.

2. Clear Communication:

Make sure that everyone in the team is aware of the team's culture and ideals. Free exchange of ideas can facilitate understanding among all parties.

3. Feedback Mechanism:

Establish a system of feedback that enables team members to voice issues and influence the culture of the team.

4. Honor Achievements:

Honor and celebrate both individual and group accomplishments. Honor those in the team who best represent the culture and ideals of the group.

The Path to Achievement.

In "How to Build a 7-Figure Real Estate Team," we offer in-depth advice on creating the appropriate values and team culture for your real estate company. It's about building a team that performs exceptionally well, adheres to strong values, and reaches the seven-figure milestone. Recall that the core of your success is in your team's culture and values as you proceed on your journey.

Part II: Building Your Brand

Chapter 3: Branding Your Real Estate Team

Creating a Distinctive Brand for Your Real Estate Team.

Your most precious asset in the cutthroat real estate market is your brand. It stands for the homes you sell as well as the assurance that your customers will have a remarkable experience. Developing a brand that appeals to your target market is essential to building a seven-figure real estate team. The art of branding your real estate team is examined in this chapter of "How to Build a 7-Figure Real Estate Team," along with its critical role in your success.

The Fundamentals of Branding.

Your brand is more than only your catchphrase, color scheme, or logo. It's the unquantifiable impact and standing your real estate team has within the community and among clients. Your team's distinctive attributes, mission, and core beliefs are all part of your brand, which makes them stand out from the competitors.

The Influence of a Potent Brand.

1. Credibility:

A powerful brand increases credibility and trust. Customers are more inclined to select a real estate group with a reputable and well-established brand.

2. Recognition:

In a congested market, a well-known brand sticks out. Ensuring that your team remains in the minds of clients and

prospects increases the likelihood that they
will recommend or return for your
services.

3. Attracting Talent:

Bringing in top talent to your team also
requires a strong brand. Professionals in
real estate are more willing to join a team
that has a solid reputation as a brand.

Developing Your Brand's Tale.

The narrative that encapsulates the history,
beliefs, and mission of your team is called
your brand story. It explains the
motivation behind your real estate
pursuits. Think of telling a tale that
illustrates your dedication to your clients'
needs and how you go above and beyond
to fulfill their aspirations. For example,
share a tale of how your staff went above

and beyond to help a client who had nearly given up discover the ideal property.

Visual Character and Uniformity. One of the most important aspects of your brand is a consistent visual identity. This covers the font, color scheme, logo, and other design components. Your brand's visual identity should be reflected in all marketing materials, including business cards and websites. Maintaining consistency throughout different channels helps to keep your brand credible and identifiable.

Consumer-First Branding. The customer experience should be the focal point of your brand. Tell your staff about happy clients who have discovered their ideal residences. Emphasize your dedication to providing individualized service, whether it's guiding first-time buyers through the process or supporting investors in growing their holdings. You may strengthen the promise of your brand by demonstrating the results of your client-centric strategy.

Developing a Seven-Figure Brand. It takes more than just numbers to be a 7-figure real estate team—it takes reputation, trust, and outstanding service. As you read "How to Build a 7-Figure Real Estate Team," keep in mind that creating a strong visual identity and brand narrative is a crucial first step toward success. Your brand is more than just a logo; it's what will make your team stand out in the real estate industry and represents your commitment to your clients.

Additionally Your brand is your North Star on the path to "How to Build a 7-Figure Real Estate Team," pointing the way toward success in a crowded and cutthroat market. It's more than just a name or a logo; it's what defines your team and sets you apart from the competition. Let's examine the craft of branding with the help of an actual incident that demonstrates the influence of a strong brand identity.

The Story of Riverside Realty: A Victory in Branding.

There was a real estate company called Riverside Realty located in the center of a busy city. Like many others, they began by trying to establish themselves in the cutthroat real estate industry. However, their dedication to creating a brand that connected with its customers was what made them stand out.

Identifying The Core.

The team members had a soul-searching session before setting out on their mission. They came to see that their core purpose was to assist families in finding their ideal home—a location where they could create lasting memories and bright futures—rather than just a place to live.

This essence turned, became their compass.

A Brand With Voice.

Riverside Realty had a slogan that really captured this spirit: "Where Dreams Find Home." More than simply words, it was a pledge to their clients that they would stop at nothing to realize their aspirations.

Continuity in Behavior.

The group realized that consistency is more important to a brand than merely having a logo. To showcase their new brand, they completely redesigned their office space, marketing collateral, and website. Their clients were left with a lasting melody in their heads because of the harmonious combination of colors, fonts, and pictures.

Prioritizing Clients.

The success of Riverside Realty was interwoven with the experiences of its clients. The Smith family, who had nearly given up on finding their ideal home, was the subject of one particularly memorable story. The Smiths were inconsolable when they discovered the property thanks to the team's unwavering dedication. The narrative of their voyage became a pillar of the Riverside Realty brand.

Smart on Social Media.

A brand's influence reaches the digital sphere. Riverside Realty made a significant social media presence investment, including not only listings but also client testimonials. The touching story of a military family discovering a warm home went viral, stirring up feelings and increasing the relatability of their brand.

The Seven-Figure Label.

As Riverside Realty grew and prospered, they realized that reputation and trust were just as important to their brand as sales figures. People trusted the brand they had established. For their clientele, the idea of "Where Dreams Find Home" had come true, and this brand had helped or aided them to grow into a seven-figure firm in the real estate industry.

Your Trip Starts Here.

As you set out to learn "Building a 7-Figure Team in real estate," keep Riverside Realty's success narrative in mind. Branding is seen as an identity that customers and Clients can identify with and trust, not just a marketing tactic. Create a memorable visual identity, tell a gripping brand story, and prioritize your customers. Your most valuable tool on this journey will be your brand.

Building a Robust or a Well Grounded Brand Identity: Boosting Your Property Group.

Creating a signature that people trust and know right away is similar to developing a strong brand identity. According to Building a 7-Figure Team in real estate, the cornerstone of your success is your brand identity. Here, we'll explore the fundamental components of an engaging brand identity that don't require a narrative.

1. Identify your central beliefs:
Knowing your team's basic beliefs clearly is the first step towards developing your brand identity. What values do you

uphold? Which values direct your behavior? Selling real estate isn't the only thing you do; you also need to provide your clients with an experience that reflects your beliefs. Your target audience and your team should share these values.

2. Establish a Distinctive Visual Identity:

The visual components that comprise your brand identity are your logo, color scheme, typography, and images. These components ought to be memorable, unique, and consistent with your principles. The core of your brand should be captured in the logo, and the appropriate feelings should be evoked by the color and font choices. In this context, expert graphic design can be quite helpful.

3. Create an Effective Tagline:
In only a few lines, a well-written tagline may communicate the promise and mission of your team. It ought to be memorable, understandable, and consistent with your basic beliefs. Your tagline has the power to become your brand's voice, speaking to customers and summarizing your values.

4. Uniformity Throughout Channels:
The secret to brand awareness is consistency. All platforms of communication, which includes your website, social media accounts, marketing materials, and even your actual office space, should use your brand identity consistently. Credibility and trust are enhanced by consistency.

5. Client-Centric Approach:

You should highlight your client-centric approach in your brand identity. It's about how you can help your clients realize their dreams, not just about you. The advantages and value you offer to your clients should be communicated through your messaging and visuals.

6. Tell Your Story:

Although one need not use a narrative in this instance, the core of your brand identity frequently derives from the tale of your team's experiences and core principles. Clients are drawn to authenticity and a personal connection that may be established by sharing your story with your audience.

7. Change with Your Audience:
Your brand identity might need to change as your real estate team expands and changes. To make sure your brand stays relevant, keep an eye out for your audience's shifting preferences and be prepared to make improvements.

8. Seek Professional Advice:
If developing a powerful brand identity feels overwhelming, think about consulting experts. Experts in marketing and graphic design can offer priceless knowledge and skills in creating a distinctive brand.

Recall that your brand identity serves as a symbol of your team's values, mission, and dedication to your clients in addition to being a marketing tool. Developing a strong brand identity is a crucial step on your path to becoming a seven-figure real estate company.

Visibility Marketing Strategies Marketing Techniques for Visibility: Developing the Brand of Your Real Estate Team.

Building a seven-figure team in the cutthroat real estate industry requires more than simply providing the greatest services—it also requires establishing a strong, recognizable brand. Here, we'll look at practical marketing techniques that will raise brand awareness and recognition without a narrative.

1. Online Presence and SEO:
In the current digital era, having a strong online presence is essential. Make sure

your group has an informative, user-friendly website that receives good search engine rankings. The foundation of internet visibility is search engine optimization, or SEO. Make good content, incorporate pertinent keywords, and optimize your website for local search results.

2. Content Marketing:

When it comes to drawing in and keeping customers, content is king. Post educational and entertaining information on a regular basis to demonstrate your expertise and give value to your audience. Examples of this type of content include blog posts, articles, and videos. Use your social media accounts and website to spread the word about this content.

3. Social Media Engagement:

Make the most of social media sites to establish a connection with prospective customers. Make sure your accounts on social media sites like Facebook, Instagram, and LinkedIn are up to date. Connect with your followers, post educational material, and use these platforms to promote your listings.

4. Email Marketing:

Email marketing is an affordable means of maintaining contact with your customers. Create a mailing list and distribute updates on market trends or newsletters. Make sure your emails are thoughtfully written, uniquely yours, and not unduly commercial.

5. Online Testimonials and Reviews:
Satisfied customers' positive remarks and reviews can greatly increase the reputation of your business. Motivate satisfied customers to post reviews on Yelp, Google My Business, and Zillow. Display these reviews on your website to attract new customers.

6. Networking and Partnerships:
Forming connections with other real estate sector experts, such as mortgage brokers, attorneys, and house inspectors, can help you grow your network and get useful recommendations.

7. Paid Advertising:
Take into account pay-per-click (PPC) advertisements on Facebook Ads and Google Ads. These ads target particular

demographics and phrases to swiftly
increase your presence.

8. Community Involvement:

Take part in neighborhood organizations,
volunteer, or sponsor events to show your
support for your community. Participating
actively in your community can improve
the perception of your brand.

9. Mobile Optimization:

Make sure your marketing materials and
website are responsive to mobile devices.
A mobile-optimized presence is crucial for
visibility because many clients use their
mobile devices to search for properties.

10. Analyze and Adjust:

Assess your marketing strategy'
effectiveness on a regular basis. Track
website traffic, email open rates, and

social media interaction with analytics tools. Adapt your tactics in response to the data to boost visibility and lead creation over time.

Recall that the purpose of these marketing techniques is to establish a reputable brand that customers would use to buy or sell real estate, not only to attract attention. These strategies will put you on the right track to building a seven-figure real estate team.

Gaining Your Audience's Trust
Developing Audience Trust: The Foundation of Real Estate Branding

In the very competitive real estate market, gaining the trust of your audience is not only crucial, but also the cornerstone of successful brand establishment. Now, without a plot, let's explore the important idea of trust-building.

1. Honesty and Transparency:
Being honest ought to be your guiding concept if you want to gain your audience's trust. Be open and honest about the skills, background, and possible shortcomings of your real estate team. One's reputation might be damaged by making excessive promises and falling short of them.

2. Consistency in Communication:
Trust and familiarity are fostered by consistent branding and communication. Make sure that the messaging on your website and social media accounts reflects the promises and values of your business.

3. Outstanding Customer Service:

A lasting impression is created by exceptional customer service. React promptly, pay close attention, and show real interest in the demands of your clients. Going above and beyond might help you develop brand ambassadors.

4. Knowledge and Expertise:
It's critical for real estate professionals to highlight their knowledge and expertise. Use webinars, in-person lectures, or blog postings to impart your knowledge. Your reputation is increased if you are a thought leader in your industry.

5. Credible Online Presence:
Maintaining an active social media presence and a professional, up-to-date website are essential for creating trust. To support your claims, include case studies,

client endorsements, and pertinent credentials.

6. Security and Privacy:

Customers demand reassurance regarding the security of their personal data. Invest in safe data handling procedures and a secure website, and make it clear that you are committed to preserving their privacy.

7. Integrity in Transactions:

During the course of negotiations and transactions, trust is frequently gained or lost. Make sure that everything is done as fairly and with the highest integrity possible, leaving no room for question.

8. Active Listening:

When you listen to your clients actively, you are demonstrating your sincere concern for their needs. To create a long-lasting relationship, pay attention to their needs, wants, and feedback and take appropriate action or response.

9. Timely Communication:

It's essential to communicate promptly in the quick-paced real estate business. Being prompt in your responses shows reliability, whether it's a response to a question or an update on a transaction.

10. Integrity in Marketing:

Steer clear of deceptive advertising strategies. In your real estate listings, tell the truth, give precise details, and avoid any dishonest tactics that can tarnish the credibility of your business.

11. Social Responsibility:

Showing that you are dedicated to having a positive influence can be accomplished by taking part in community events or donating to local causes.

12. Client Education:

Inform your clients about the procedure involved in buying a home. Clients that are knowledgeable are more inclined to accept your advice and suggestions.

13. Regular Follow-Up:

Relationship maintenance doesn't stop with a sale. Reminding former customers on a regular basis demonstrates your respect for their business and confidence.

14. Reliability and Follow-Through:

The credibility of your brand is based on how well you keep your word. Make sure you honor your promises on a regular basis.

Gaining the trust of your audience is a continuous process that is frequently facilitated by a succession of satisfying encounters and exchanges. You can build a brand that clients rely on and trust by continuously using these concepts, which will eventually lead to the creation of a seven-figure real estate team.

Chapter 4.

Leveraging Technology and Tools

The saying ***"knowledge is power"*** has taken on a new meaning in the dynamic real estate market: "knowledge, wielded through technology, is paramount." Let's examine, using an engaging narrative, how technology and tools are essential to developing your brand.

Sarah, an experienced broker in the fast-paced real estate industry, had dreamed of growing her small, dedicated team into a seven-figure juggernaut. Sarah realized she needed to embrace the digital world in order to turn her idea into a reality. With unwavering resolve, she set out on a mission to use tools and technology to elevate her brand to unprecedented heights.

1. Digital Presence and Online Visibility: Sarah understood that your online presence serves as the face of your brand in the digital era. She made an investment in a modern, easy-to-use website that displayed her listings, market analysis, and useful links. With the newest listings, virtual tours, and educational blog entries, her website swiftly established itself as a central point for prospective customers.

The takeaway: The cornerstone of contemporary branding is a robust web presence. As your online business, your website should serve as more than just a digital brochure.

2. Systems for Managing Customer Relationships (CRM):

Sarah embraced a powerful CRM system in order to stay up to date with client interactions and sustain customized partnerships. It enabled her to keep tabs on customer preferences, foresee their requirements, and deliver individualized service.

The takeaway: A CRM system is a tool for fostering connections and providing top-notch customer service, not merely for monitoring contacts.

3. 3D Tours and Virtual Reality:

Sarah became aware of the real estate industry's potential for virtual reality and 3D tours. Her listings allowed clients to view properties from the comfort of their homes thanks to the integration of these state-of-the-art technologies.

The takeaway: Adopt technology that improves customer satisfaction and makes it simpler for customers to interact with your business.

4. Social Media Marketing:
Sarah saw social media's potential. She became well-known on social media sites including LinkedIn, Instagram, and Facebook. By disseminating captivating information, highlighting industry trends, and presenting success stories, she broadened her audience and personally connected with prospective customers.

The takeaway: Social media is an effective tool for branding and isn't merely for fostering personal relationships. Make use of it to establish a human connection with your audience and showcase your business.

5. Data Analytics and Market Insights:

Sarah used the power of insights by utilizing cutting-edge data analytics techniques. She was able to foresee market trends, customize her listings, and provide clients with insightful counsel.

The takeaway: Your brand benefits from data-driven decision-making. Make use of tools to improve your market knowledge and service delivery.

6. SEO and Online Advertising:

Sarah made an investment in search engine optimization and online advertising. She made sure her brand was exposed to potential customers at the proper time by implementing effective ad campaigns and selecting the right keywords.

The takeaway: Search engine optimization and online advertising can greatly increase your brand's visibility and draw in prospective customers who are actively looking for real estate services. Sarah's tale is one of change, propelled by the astute application of tools and technology.

These components are not simply possibilities in the digital age; they are essential for any real estate company hoping to grow a seven-figure staff. You may strengthen your brand, provide better service to your clients, and achieve new levels of success in the cutthroat real estate industry by utilizing these tools.

Technology's Place in Real Estate: Shaking Up the Success Path

Technology is a key factor that is influencing the real estate industry's rapidly changing landscape. The days of using antiquated techniques are long gone, as today's top real estate agents leverage technology to improve customer relations, expedite workflows, and eventually create seven-figure real estate teams. Let's examine the many facets of technology's involvement in real estate and how it supports the success of your brand.

1. Increased Efficiency:

Real estate activities are now considerably more efficient thanks to technological advancements. Technology saves time-consuming human processes, from digitizing paperwork and automating mundane activities to streamlining the search for properties. Real estate agents that are efficient not only save time but also have the capacity to manage more deals, which raises their chances of success.

2. Big Data and Analytics:

Technology has facilitated the quicker access to and analysis of information, which is crucial in the data-driven real estate sector. The utilization of big data and analytics techniques yields significant insights into customer behavior, market trends, and property prices. With these insights at their disposal, real estate agents may optimize their strategies, make well-informed judgments, and meet the changing demands of their clientele.

3. Enhanced Client Interaction:
The foundation of any prosperous real estate team is strong client interaction. Real estate agents can now establish stronger connections with their clients because of technology. With the help of immersive experiences like virtual property tours, 3D walkthroughs, and video conferences, clients can make well-informed selections without ever leaving their homes. By keeping agents available and responsive, real-time communication tools foster strong client connections.

4. Marketing and Branding:
Utilizing technology provides a plethora of tools to accomplish efficient marketing techniques, which are essential to developing a strong real estate brand. Brand exposure is made possible by social

media platforms, email marketing, and internet advertising. Via eye-catching material, real estate agents can introduce their knowledge and listings to a larger audience.

5. Flexibility and Mobility:

In the real estate sector, mobility is revolutionary. Cloud-based platforms and mobile apps enable real estate agents to operate remotely. They offer flexibility that fits with the current lifestyle by enabling them to access listings, contracts, and client information while on the road.

6. Safety and Security:

Real estate technology also takes safety and security into account. Properties are equipped with smart lock technology, video monitoring, and state-of-the-art security systems to safeguard both tenants and brokers.

7. Competitive Advantage:
Technology can give a big advantage in a field where competition is fierce. Those in the real estate industry that keep up with the latest technological advancements will have an advantage over their competitors. They are also more likely to draw in and keep customers if they adjust to shifting consumer tastes.

Technology is a force that is transforming the real estate industry, not just a tool. It gives real estate agents the ability to work more productively, interact with clients in a meaningful way, and build a powerful online presence. Knowing how technology works is essential when you set out to create a seven-figure real estate team. You will succeed in the dynamic real estate market if you embrace it as a central tenet of your approach.

Essential Apps and Software Real Estate Essential Apps and Software: Build a 7-Figure Team

Using technology and the appropriate software and apps are crucial stages in creating a profitable seven-figure real estate team in the fast-paced real estate industry. These tools assist you in building a strong brand presence in addition to streamlining company operations. Let's examine the crucial tools and technologies that can revolutionize your real estate company.

1. Software for Customer Relationship Management (CRM):

The foundation of any real estate business is CRM software. You can track leads, handle client relations, and keep an extensive database using it. CRMs that provide you a 360-degree perspective of your customers, such as Salesforce, Zoho, and HubSpot, let you customize your offerings to meet their unique requirements. Additionally, many platforms have automation features that make follow-up and communication easier.

2. Listing Management Platforms:

For real estate agents, listing management solutions like property management software and MLS connections are essential. You can effectively generate, edit, and distribute property listings with these systems. Applications such as Brokermint and Dotloop help securely manage documents, contracts, and transactions in the digital world.

3. Apps for Virtual Tours and 3D Visualization:

Adding virtual tours and 3D visualizations to your property listings is a great method to draw in buyers. With the use of apps like Matterport and EyeSpy360, you can create interactive, immersive property tours from the comfort of your home for prospective buyers.

4. Marketing and Social Media Tools:

Establishing your brand online requires a strong online presence. By scheduling and analyzing your social media postings, you may reach a wider audience with social media management tools like Hootsuite and Buffer. You can produce eye-catching content for your listings and marketing materials with Adobe Creative Cloud.

5. Platforms for Collaboration and Communication:

It's critical to have effective client and team communication. Slack and Microsoft Teams are two examples of apps that improve teamwork by making sure that everyone is in agreement. Remote work is more productive when virtual meetings are facilitated by video conferencing apps like Zoom and Google Meet.

6. Real Estate Professional Mobile Apps:

These apps provide on-the-go access to listings, contracts, and client data for real estate professionals. For example, Zillow and Redfin offer real-time property information, and DocuSign and HelloSign facilitate e-signature transactions by streamlining the procedure.

7. Tools for Market Research and Data Analytics:

Making decisions based on data is crucial for real estate success. Comprehensive market data and analytics are provided by tools like RealScout and Realtors Property Resource (RPR), which assist you in recognizing trends and coming to wise judgments.

8. Photo Editing Programs and Virtual Staging Tools:

While photo editing programs like Canva and Adobe Lightroom improve the aesthetic appeal of your listings, virtual staging tools let you turn empty houses into hospitable residences.

9. Customer care and Support Apps:
Bcing able to provide quick customer care makes you stand out from the crowd. You may successfully manage client questions and support with the use of apps like Zendesk and Freshdesk.

10. Internet Reviews and Reputation Management:
It's important to manage your online image. You can keep an eye on and manage online reviews and client feedback with the use of tools like Podium and BirdEye.

Your real estate company will run more smoothly and establish a strong brand presence if you integrate these necessary tools and technologies. Using the newest technologies and embracing technology can set you up for success as you strive to develop a seven-figure real estate team. With the help of these digital resources, you can maintain your edge in the always changing real estate market, effectively engage customers, and build a reputation for yourself.

Optimizing Productivity
Efficiency Maximization: Unlocking Real Estate Technology's Full Potential.

Success in the fast-paced real estate industry frequently depends on efficiency. Having the correct tools and technology can greatly improve your capacity to develop your brand, optimize your processes, and eventually grow a seven-figure real estate team.

Now let's explore the methods for utilizing technology to increase efficiency:

1. Your Ally is Automation:
Automation is one of real estate technology's most potent advantages. It frees up time for more important duties by enabling you to complete everyday tasks with little effort. Automate follow-up messages, appointment scheduling, and email responses by utilizing customer relationship management (CRM) solutions. By using marketing automation solutions, you can save hours of manual labor by providing clients with individualized content and listings.

2. Making Decisions Based on Data:
Powerful data analytics technologies offer insightful information about customer preferences, market trends, and listing performance. You can more effectively

allocate resources, concentrate on high-value prospects, and customize your tactics by utilizing this information. For example, you might focus your marketing efforts in an area if analytics show a spike in demand for a particular type of property.

3. Remote Work and Virtual Collaboration:

Traditional office spaces are no longer the exclusive domain for the real estate industry. You can do business from anywhere with the help of remote work and virtual collaboration tools, giving you the flexibility you need to serve a wider clientele. Clients and team members can collaborate effortlessly thanks to secure cloud storage, document-sharing platforms, and video conferencing. You can clinch deals, facilitate contract negotiations, and provide virtual property tours with these tools—all without having to hold in-person meetings.

4. Simplified Transaction Management: Managing agreements, paperwork, and transactions is a significant aspect of real estate. This procedure is made simpler by transaction management software, which centralizes papers, digitizes paperwork, and assures compliance. It streamlines the closing process and lowers errors, giving clients a more positive experience.

5. Enhanced Marketing Capabilities: Establishing your brand in the real estate industry starts with effective marketing. To reach more people, make use of software for social media management, email marketing, and internet advertising. These tools let you target particular groups, monitor the effectiveness of campaigns, and make real-time adjustments to your marketing tactics.

6. Mobile Solutions for Agents on the Go:

Real estate agents are never stationary. Agents may use their smartphones or tablets to browse listings, interact with clients, and handle transactions thanks to industry-specific mobile apps. This mobility gives you a competitive edge in swiftly responding to client questions, in addition to saving time.

7. Digital Signature Solutions:

Documents are no longer printed, signed, and scanned. Clients can sign documents more easily and securely from any location with the help of digital signature systems. When it comes to shortening the time it takes to close deals, this technology is revolutionary.

8. 3D Visualization and Virtual Tours: Real estate requires eye-catching imagery. Tools for virtual tours and 3D visualization enable prospective purchasers to view houses from a distance. By doing this, both parties save time and can be sure that potential buyers are sincere in their interest before ever seeing the property.

Using these technologies to your advantage is the key to maximizing the efficiency of your real estate operations through technology. You may increase client satisfaction, boost productivity, and establish yourself as a tech-savvy, effective real estate team by doing this. Accept these improvements, and you'll be

well on your way to becoming a
successful seven-figure real estate agent.

Part III: Lead Generation and Conversion

Chapter 5: Effective Lead Generation Strategies

Powerful Lead Generation Techniques: The Foundation of Your Seven-Figure Real Estate Group.

Effective lead creation in the real estate industry is like hitting gold. It is essential to your company's survival and the secret to developing a seven-figure real estate team. Let's examine how utilizing powerful lead generation techniques with an engaging narrative might elevate your real estate endeavors.

Once upon a time, Sarah, a real estate agent, resided in the busy city of

Metropolis. She was driven to become a seven-figure real estate team owner and accomplish extraordinary achievement. Sarah was aware that her capacity to efficiently produce leads was the cornerstone of her desire.

Metropolis was renowned for its varied neighborhoods, each possessing its own allure and personality. Sarah made the decision to take advantage of this diversity. She vividly brought the stories of the neighborhoods she worked in to life by crafting a compelling story around them. She communicated the fascinating local hotspots, cultural attractions, and rich history that characterized each community through intriguing social media postings and blog entries.

People in Metropolis started to regard Sarah as a reliable source of local information in addition to a real estate agent. Her genuine narrative fostered a feeling of community and attracted online shoppers and vendors. She was regarded by them as the city's foremost authority on real estate.

Sarah's list of leads grew along with her reputation. She was aware that drawing customers who were actually interested in the city and its districts required using the storytelling technique. These were the leads who valued the real, heartfelt bond she had established.

Sarah also used technology well to gather leads. Visitors to her website could see market reports, examine properties, and take 3D virtual tours thanks to interactive technologies. Visitors gave Sarah their contact information in exchange for this useful information, which she used to foster relationships.

She was aware of the significance of niche marketing. She created client personas by analyzing their surfing habits and interests, and then used this information to craft offers and communications that spoke to each lead individually. Her conversion rate shot through the roof, converting inquisitive visitors into enthusiastic customers.

Sarah, though, didn't stop there. She understood the value of lead nurturing and follow-up. She made sure to respond to leads as soon as possible, answering their questions and helping them with the process of buying or selling a house. She had a stellar reputation because of her promptness and sincere concern.

Sarah's seven-figure real estate team eventually came to be. Her tale involved more than just sales; it involved creating a neighborhood of contented homeowners. She had become an expert at creating leads using technology, storytelling, and authenticity rather than forceful marketing.

Sarah's journey in Metropolis shows us that building strong connections is just as important to successful lead generation as quantity. Technology used in conjunction with a compelling tale can convert indifferent people into devoted customers. You're creating a legacy with these lead generation techniques in addition to a real estate staff.

A true commitment to developing relationships, technological prowess, and strategic storytelling come together in a dynamic process that is effective lead generation. You too can become an expert at these tactics and build a successful seven-figure real estate team that makes a lasting impression in your market, just like Sarah did in our tale.

Additionally, lead generation is the business's lifeblood in the real estate industry. It is the skill of not only locating possible customers but also converting those leads into devoted lifelong supporters. As you set out to develop a seven-figure real estate team, successful lead generation techniques will be essential to your success.

1.Adopt Digital Marketing:

Your website serves as your storefront in the modern digital era. Invest in a business website that is mobile-friendly, aesthetically pleasing, and easy to navigate. Present your property listings and ensure that guests may get in touch with you with ease. Use search engine optimization (SEO) to your advantage to make sure your website shows up prominently in search results, which will make it simpler for prospective customers to locate you.

2. Utilize Social Media:

Social media sites are useful resources for real estate agents, not simply for personal use. Make interesting accounts on social media sites such as LinkedIn, Instagram, and Facebook. To reach potential customers, post high-quality pictures and videos of your listings, interact with your audience, and launch focused advertising campaigns. Keeping an active social media presence requires consistency.

3. Content is King in Content Marketing: Provide insightful content to establish oneself as an informed and reliable resource in the real estate sector. Publish educational articles about real estate investment, purchasing, and selling in a blog on your website. Post educational content to interact with your audience and share your knowledge on social media.

4. Email marketing:
Getting in touch with potential customers via email is still one of the best strategies. Create a contact list and deliver interesting newsletters on a regular basis. Provide real estate listings, market updates, and

insightful advice. Make your emails
unique to the interests and requirements of
your leads.

5. Lead magnets:

Provide a valuable offer in return for a
contact list. Make e-books, market studies,
or property guides as lead magnets.
Potential customers that download these
materials provide you with quality leads
that you can add to your database.

6. Real Estate Lead Generation
Software: To maximize efficiency, make
an investment in lead generation software.
You can automate follow-up procedures,
manage your database, and collect leads
with the use of these tools. They can also
supply you information about the behavior
of leads, which can help you customize
your marketing tactics.

6. Networking and Referrals:

Traditional networking has a lot of power that should not be undervalued. Engage in local business groups, go to real estate events, and network with other professionals. Urge pleased customers to recommend your services to their friends and family. Referrals from friends and family are among the most important leads you can acquire.

8. Following up and Nurturing:

Gathering leads is simply the first step. Those leads become devoted customers when they are nurtured. Create a follow-up system that involves regular interaction, tailored communication, and prompt answers to questions.

9.Utilize Data to your Advantage using Data Analytics:

Examine how well your lead creation tactics are working. Determine what is and is not working, then modify your strategy accordingly. You can find useful data for your investigation on platforms like social media insights and Google Analytics.

10. Client Testimonials:

Highlight your achievements. Urge pleased customers to post reviews on review websites and your website. Good testimonies and reviews serve as social proof, encouraging prospective customers to trust you.

Generating leads effectively is not a one-size-fits-all process. It needs constant care, a deliberate blending of offline and online activities, and a dedication to

remain ahead of the digital curve. You'll
be well on your way to developing a
seven-figure real estate team that succeeds
in a cutthroat market by putting these
techniques into practice and customizing
them for your own market.

Offline vs. Online Lead Processing Finding the Optimal Balance Between Online and Offline Lead Gen Strategies

The argument over online vs offline lead
generation frequently takes center stage
when trying to establish a seven-figure
real estate team. While some people firmly
believe in the efficacy of internet
marketing, others support more
conventional, offline approaches. The best
course of action, in actuality, is to combine
the advantages of offline and internet lead
creation.

Online Lead Creation: The Next Big Thing in Technology

1.Greater Reach:
The internet has a reach that is unmatched. By using effective web marketing techniques, you may reach potential customers both locally and beyond. Online advertising, social media profiles, and your website can pull leads from all over the internet.

2. Data-Driven Insights:
Access to a wealth of data is made possible via online lead creation. You may monitor user activity, preferences, and demographics with the use of tools like social media insights and Google Analytics. With the help of this data, you can optimize the impact of your marketing campaigns.

3. Cost-Effective:

Online marketing has the potential to be less expensive than traditional advertising. With pay-per-click (PPC) advertising, you are only required to pay when someone clicks on your ads. Email campaigns and content marketing can also be very economical.

4. Instant Engagement:

Internet-based tactics provide engagement right now. A single click can connect you with potential customers, and live chat features enable immediate interaction. This velocity is especially important in a real estate market that is moving quickly.

5. Automated Follow-Up:

Automation tools can be used in online lead generation to nurture leads. Chatbots, drip marketing, and automated email responses make sure that no lead is lost.

Lead Generation Offline: The Human Touch

1.Local Market Focus:
Offline lead generation is still a potent tool for local real estate marketplaces. You may establish a strong local presence by participating in neighborhood activities, sponsoring local causes, and networking at community events.

2. Personal Connection:
In-person conversations foster trust. It is easier to establish a personal connection with potential clients in person than it is to do it online. Dealing with people they know and trust is common.

3. Targeted Networking:

Targeted networking is frequently possible with offline means. You can establish connections with other professionals in the area who can refer you and work together. Developing connections with mortgage brokers, lawyers, and house inspectors can result in high-quality leads.

4. Tangible Marketing:

Print ads and direct mail are still valuable forms of traditional marketing. Tangible items can aid prospective customers in remembering your offerings and getting in touch with you when they're ready.

5. Word-of-Mouth:

marketing and referrals are frequent outcomes of offline interactions. Encourage happy customers to tell their friends and family about your offerings.

These leads are frequently pre-qualified and of a good caliber.

Getting Balance: A Comprehensive Method

The most prosperous real estate agents recognize the need of integrating offline and internet lead creation techniques. While offline approaches offer the human touch and local market presence, online methods offer a wider reach and data-driven insights. Developing a complete plan that capitalizes on the advantages of both domains is crucial.

Online advertising, for instance, can send leads to your website, where they can learn more about your involvement in the community and the individualized attention you provide. Networking in person has the potential to generate internet contacts and follow-ups. Recall that members of your target audience might interact through offline and online channels. Consequently, developing a seven-figure real estate team necessitates a comprehensive strategy that acknowledges the significance of finding the ideal balance between the digital and real worlds. Social media, content marketing, and SEO

The Digital Triad of Social Media, SEO, and Content Marketing for Efficient Lead Generation.

To create a real estate team that generates seven figures, it is essential to become an expert in digital lead generation. Although offline and online approaches are equally important, there are a wealth of options in the digital space. Social networking, content marketing, and SEO (Search Engine Optimization) are some of your most effective tools.

1. Search Engine Optimization, or SEO: The foundation of your internet presence is SEO. It's the deliberate craft of optimizing your content and website for search engines. This is the reason it's vital:

Visibility is Key: Potential customers use search engines like Google to find real estate services. A high search engine ranking ensures and guarantees that potential clients will see you.

Quality Leads: Search engine optimization (SEO) is premised or established on quality leads in addition to boosting your online presence. People that are looking for particular real estate services are already intrigued by what you do.

Local SEO: Get your website ready for searches in your area. To attract people who are looking for real estate services in your area, include location-specific keywords.

Quality of Content: Google favors high-quality content. You may raise your ranking by consistently posting interesting and educational content.

2. Social Networks:

Social media networks have metamorphosed into effective lead generation tools in the current digital era:

Brand Building: You can use social media to develop your brand. Building trust and familiarity across platforms is facilitated by consistent branding.

Engagement: Use social media sites like Facebook, Instagram, and LinkedIn to communicate with your followers. Distribute interesting stuff and answer messages and comments. Interaction fosters relationships that may result in high-quality leads.

Paid Advertising: You can target particular demographics with the help of social media networks' paid advertising alternatives. It's a useful strategy for attracting new customers.

Making the Most of Visual Content: Visual content is predominant on sites like Pinterest and Instagram. Use these to distribute pictures and videos of your properties. Lead generation can be greatly impacted by visual material.

3. Promotion of Content: When it comes to digital, content is king. Produce informational yet captivating and persuasive content:

Blogging: Keep a blog running on your website. You can establish yourself as a real estate authority by frequently posting blog entries that answer frequently asked questions and issues.

Educational Materials: Provide materials like guides, whitepapers, and eBooks in return for contact details. You generate leads and develop authority by doing this.

Email Campaigns: Send out emails that are fueled by your content. Prospective customers will remember you if you send out regular newsletters, market updates, and property highlights.

Video Content: Educational real estate movies and property tours make for very interesting viewing. Social media and websites like YouTube are ideal for distributing video content.

The Digital Triad's Synergy: While each of these digital technologies is strong on its own, when used in tandem, they provide a potent force for lead generation. One practical tactic could be to use SEO to drive visitors to your website. When they get there, they interact with your material and are urged to follow you on social media. Their attention is piqued by social media activity and the useful information your blog offers.

In the digital age, these tools are indispensable, but don't underestimate the value of a well-rounded approach. For the best strategy for creating a seven-figure real estate team, combine them with offline techniques like word-of-mouth recommendations and local networking.

Finding the ideal balance between these digital factors and conventional methods allows lead generation and conversion to become dynamic, efficient, and very effective processes.

Connections and Suggestions
Referrals and Networking: A Reliable Route to Lead Creation

It's simple to undervalue the importance of networking and referrals in the digital age, when internet marketing tactics frequently take the lead in real estate marketing. Still, word-of-mouth recommendations, in-person contacts, and personal relationships are vital resources when trying to assemble a seven-figure real estate team. Here's why these techniques are not just pertinent, but essential:

1. Establishing Relationships:

Building relationships is essential to success in the real estate market. Through networking, one can establish sincere relationships with clients, other professionals, and possible leads. The connections you make at industry events, neighborhood get-togethers, or social activities can serve as the cornerstone for your lead generation.

2. Confidence and Credibility:

The real estate industry uses trust as its currency. Through networking, you can forge enduring connections and develop your credibility. Credibility is what gives customers confidence in their decision, and trust is what draws them to your services.

3. Word-of-mouth Recommendations: Suggestions from contented customers are invaluable. Someone is almost endorsing you when they refer a friend or family member to you. These leads are frequently pre-qualified and prepared to interact, which improves the effectiveness of your conversion process.

4. Reaching Markets: Networking gives you access to possible leads and niche markets that traditional online marketing might not be able to reach. One way to network with homeowners who aren't actively looking for a property right now but might be in the future is to go to local community gatherings.

5. Business Collaborations: Working together with other experts in the field, such mortgage brokers, real estate lawyers, and house inspectors, might lead to new prospects for lead creation. These alliances establish a network in which suggestions and referrals come easily.

Effective Networking Strategies: Take into Account the Following Tactics to Maximize Referrals and Networking:

Prioritize Quality Over Quantity

Rather than accumulating a large number of contacts, concentrate on creating a smaller network of superior relationships. The depth of these connections is what will result in significant recommendations.

• Be a Resource: Don't use networking as a way to obtain leads only. Have a sincere desire to be of service, impart information, and assist people. People will then be more inclined to recommend you to others.

Regular Follow-Up

Continue to communicate with your network on a regular basis. Maintain social media connections, give sporadic calls, and send follow-up emails. By doing this, your relationships remain vibrant and new.

Professional Development

Participate in conferences, seminars, and workshops relevant to your field. This will provide you plenty of chances to meet possible leads in addition to enhancing your knowledge.

Online Presence

Make the most of your online presence, particularly on business-oriented websites like LinkedIn. Talk to prospective clients and coworkers, share your knowledge, and participate in conversations. Although there are unquestionable benefits to online lead creation, networking and personal recommendations can offer a special and powerful advantage. Creating a strong and well-rounded lead generation system through the effective integration of traditional and digital marketing techniques is essential to building a seven-figure real estate team.

Chapter 6.

Converting Leads into Clients

Suppose you have implemented a comprehensive lead generating plan, and as a result, your email is now overflowing with questions and prospective prospects. Even though you should be happy about this, you are only now starting down the path to creating a seven-figure real estate team. When you turn those leads into partners, advocates, and clients, that's when the true magic happens.

The Conversion Art:
In the real estate industry, conversion is a fine art that calls for a combination of market expertise, emotional intelligence, and communication abilities. Encouraging

prospective clients to book or select you as their real estate agent also involves assisting them in their decision-making process and instilling confidence in them.

The Story of Lead Conversion: Allow me to tell you a tale that demonstrates the value of successful lead conversion: Introducing Jane, a motivated buyer who recently enquired about one of your listed properties. She is naturally cautious, but she is also anxious to find her ideal home. She has a lot of doubts and questions, which she conveys in her first message to you.

This is where your abilities are put to use. You answer quickly and kindly, addressing Jane's worries with knowledge and compassion. You set up a face-to-face appointment and promise to guide her through the entire procedure. It's during the first meeting when you really shine. You're ready, demonstrating your in-depth familiarity with the neighborhood real estate market and your commitment to assisting Jane in locating or finding the ideal building or house. She feels appreciated and heard when you actively listen to her needs and worries.

Over the course of the weeks, you lead Jane on property tours, give insightful commentary, and competent guidance. You ease her hesitations and fears by being a constant source of communication and open exchange of information. When Jane finally finds the house of her dreams, you help her through the closing process with ease and make sure she has a hassle-free experience. Jane is pleased with her purchase and finds your commitment to be impressive. She not only turns into a happy customer but also a fervent supporter of your offerings. Her recommendations of her friends and family grow your clientele.

Crucial Techniques for a Winning Conversion:

1. Active Listening:

It's critical to comprehend the wants, needs, and problems of your lead. Active listening is the first step in this throughout your early conversations.

2. Education and Openness:

Customers value experts who help them navigate intricate procedures and offer insightful advice. Communicate your expertise while remaining open-minded at all times.

3. Prompt and Consistent Communication: Establish confidence by being dependable and providing prompt answers and follow-ups.

4. Personalized Approach: Since each client is different, it's critical to customize your services to meet their needs. Avoid adopting a one-size-fits-all strategy.

5. Controlling Expectations: There will inevitably be ups and downs in real estate deals. Stress and anxiety can be decreased by controlling your clients' expectations and providing them with information.

In conclusion, conversion is about giving your clients a smooth and fulfilling experience rather than merely sealing a purchase. You may convert prospects into partners by keeping things transparent, concentrating on the needs of each individual lead, and assisting leads along the way. These contented customers will not only help you grow into a seven-figure real estate team but also turn into your strongest supporters within the business.

Additionally Converting leads into clients is similar to turning prospects into valuable partners in the real estate industry. This procedure is an art that calls for dexterity, skill, and commitment; it is not just a transaction. Learning the art of lead conversion becomes essential to your success when you set out to create a seven-figure real estate team.

Here is a thorough tutorial on how to become proficient in this crucial ability.

The Craft of Converting:
There are many more steps involved in turning a lead into a client than simply closing a contract. It's about developing a relationship, earning their trust, and making sure prospective customers feel appreciated along the way in addition to being secure in their choice. The following are essential elements for being an expert in lead conversion:

1. Effective Communication:
Get back to them quickly: In real estate, time is of the essence. Answering questions promptly shows that you are dedicated and focused.

Active Listening: Recognize your leads' wants, needs, and worries. This lets you adjust your strategy to fit their particular circumstance.

2. Market Knowledge:

Act as the go-to person in the area for information on the market: Your leads depend on you. Present your knowledge by offering insightful data and market analysis.

3. Emotional Intelligence:

Understanding and Empathy: Recognize the emotional component of purchasing or selling a home. Acknowledge your lead's emotions and express sympathy for their worries.

4. Honesty and Transparency:

Keep lines of communication open and clear: be honest at all times. Inform your clients of all the steps involved and any obstacles that may arise.

5. Customization:

Personalized Assistance: Recognize that every customer is different. Tailor your strategy to their unique requirements and inclinations.

6. Managing Expectations:

Get Clients Ready for the Ride: Real estate deals frequently involve ups and downs. Reducing worry and preserving trust can be achieved by controlling your clients' expectations and providing them with updates.

The Conversion Process:

There is usually a set route that leads from lead to client:

1. First Contact:

This is the first exchange of information, which frequently takes the form of queries, emails, or phone calls. To make a good impression, you must respond promptly and kindly.

2. In-Depth Conversation:

Have in-depth discussions to learn about the objectives, tastes, and worries of your lead. Here's when empathy and attentive listening come into play.

3. Education and Counseling:

Share your knowledge and counsel, offering insights about the neighborhood real estate market, properties that are for sale, and the purchasing or selling procedure. Providing your expertise fosters trust.

4. Transparency: Inform your clients of any problems or hurdles that may arise.

Trust is preserved through transparency even in the face of adversity.

5. Consistent Communication:

Keep in regular contact with clients to inform them of your progress and address any queries they may have.

6. Sealing the Deal:

Your efforts will be rewarded when you successfully lead your clients through the negotiations, inspections, and closing procedure.

7. Relationship After closure:

After closure, your relationship continues. Remain in contact and offer help; happy customers can end up becoming your greatest promoters.

Important Lessons:
The art of turning leads into clients involves establishing credibility, offering knowledgeable advice, and making sure your clients have a flawless experience. Gaining proficiency in this area will enable you to support the success of your team as well as build a network of pleased customers who will recommend you to others. This is the route to building a seven-figure real estate business and being well-known in the field.

**Conversion: The Art of Mastery.
Conversion Optimization: Creating
Clients from Leads.**

The talent of turning leads into clients is what sets successful real estate agents and teams apart from the competition. It's critical to grasp the art of conversion as you work to assemble your seven-figure real estate team. In the realm of real estate transactions, ***it's not only about closing agreements;*** it's also about building enduring relationships and earning the trust of partners. Here, we explore the fundamentals of this craft and explain how it might be the secret to your success.

The Art and Science of Conversion
The process of turning leads into clients is a combination of science and art; **there is no one-size-fits-all approach.** Even when

data-driven tactics are used, people are still very important.

Here's how to become an expert at conversion:

Lead Segmentation.
Determine And Classify Your Leads:

Every lead is not created equal. Sort them according to their interests, readiness to buy or sell, and other pertinent criteria. **Personalized Approach:** Adapt your engagement and communication tactics to each segment's unique requirements and preferences.

Establishing Trust.
Honesty and Transparency:
Communicate in an open and sincere manner to establish trust. Agents that manage expectations and give factual information are valued by clients.

Demonstrate Empathy: Recognize the sentimental components of real estate deals. Show that you care about your customers' well-being in addition to making sales by demonstrating your empathy for their worries.

Skillful Interaction.

Prompt Replies: Your prompt attention to questions and issues demonstrates your dedication to your customers.

Listening intently: Pay attention to the wants, needs, and concerns of your clientele. This aids in comprehension as well as approach customization.

Expertise and Knowledge.

Gain vital insights on the local market, neighborhoods, and property values by being the go-to person in the area.

Solving Problems Proactively: Prevent impediments by anticipating and addressing such issues before they arise. Customers respect agents who can effectively handle complexity.

Individualization

Tailored Approaches: Acknowledge that every customer is different. Provide specialized solutions based on their unique needs, interests, and aspirations.
Assert your ability to recognize each client's unique needs and modify your strategy accordingly.

Efficient Conversion Route.
Simplified Procedure:

Create a well-organized route from the point of contact to the completion of the transaction. It ought to have precise steps and objectives.

Smooth Transitions: Make sure that your clients go from leads to prospects to clients in a seamless manner.

Establishing Long-Term Relationships. After-closure care: You should continue to communicate with clients after the closing. Stay in touch and keep offering assistance as their go-to real estate consultant.

Important Lessons:
Understanding the subtleties of your leads, developing trust via open and sympathetic communication, and tailoring your

approach are all necessary to become an expert in the art of conversion. You're not just converting leads when you take the time to understand each client's unique demands and tailor your services to meet those needs; you're building lifelong clients. This art and data-driven tactics will surely put you on the right track to being a leader in the real estate market and developing a seven-figure team.

The Sales Funnel: Getting From Lead to Sale

Sales Funnel: From Lead to Closing
The process from lead to client in the real estate industry is sometimes likened to a sales funnel, which is a methodical procedure that converts prospective clients into contented patrons. Any real estate agent hoping to develop a seven-figure

team must comprehend the nuances of this funnel. Let's examine the sales funnel and the steps involved in turning leads into customers in more detail:

1. Awareness:

The **"Awareness"** stage, which is the biggest portion of the funnel, is where it starts. Here, prospective customers learn about your company, offerings, or services. This could happen via a number of methods, including community involvement, online advertising, social media, and recommendations.

Your objective is to reach a broad audience and spark interest from a variety of possible customers. During this stage, compelling content and successful marketing are essential.

2. Interest:

After learning about your brand, some prospective customers will go on to the **"Interest"** phase. They appear genuinely interested in what you have to give. This can be indicated by doing things like visiting your website, signing up for emails, or going to your open houses. At this stage, offering helpful information and demonstrating your experience is crucial. Give them a cause to be curious to find out more.

3. Consideration:

Leads turn into prospects during the **"Consideration"** stage. They're currently considering you seriously to see if you're the best fit for their real estate requirements. They might speak with you directly, pose inquiries, and make requests for more details. Here, it's your responsibility to respond intelligently, allay their worries, and emphasize your advantages as a real estate expert. Honesty and openness are crucial.

4. Intent:

During the **"Intent"** phase, potential customers have developed into viable leads. They've made it plain that they want to buy or sell, and they might be looking into particulars like the property's characteristics, available financing, or the associated legal procedures.

Because potential clients are on the verge of making a decision, it is imperative to keep a sense of urgency at this point. Give them every tool they require so they can proceed with assurance.

5. Evaluation:

Applicants that advance to the **"Evaluation"** phase carefully weigh their selections. They're probably taking into account a number of real estate agents or properties.
It's your job to differentiate yourself from the crowd. Present your special selling point, highlight your experience, and provide convincing arguments for why they should pick you.

6. Purchase:

The point of conversion is indicated by the **"Purchase"** stage. The completion of a transaction turns a prospect into a client. This could entail accepting a listing, putting in an offer, or signing a contract.

Assisting the prospect in making the smooth transition from prospect to client, making sure all documentation is in line, and assisting them with the closing process are all part of your job.

7. Advocacy and Loyalty:

The funnel continues after the "Purchase" stage. In actuality, it continues well after closure. Positive client experiences can turn them into devoted patrons and brand ambassadors.
Securing long-term success requires preserving this relationship, providing post-closure support, and encouraging referrals.

Effective lead to client conversion depends on knowing and optimizing each stage of the sales funnel. Focusing on this methodical strategy will help you manage leads effectively, deliver value at every turn, and eventually reach your goals in the cutthroat real estate industry as you work to develop your seven-figure real estate team.

CRM, or customer relationship management

CRM (Customer Relationship Management):

The Conversion Catalyst

Converting leads into clients in the ever-changing real estate industry is a complex challenge. A carefully thought-out plan that blends productive lead generation with successful conversion tactics is essential for success. Customer Relationship Management (CRM), a dynamic tool that is essential to optimizing the process and growing your real estate company to seven figures, is at the center of this approach.

1. Data Collection and Management as the Basis of CRM

Thorough data management and collecting is the first step in the lead to client process. CRM systems give you a central location to keep important data about your leads, prospects, and customers. Contact details, preferences for properties, communication history, and other data might be included in this information. Being able to instantly access this data is crucial for customizing your approach to the particular requirements of each lead.

2. Customization:

The Influence of Personalized Letters

CRM solutions facilitate focused and customized communication. You may send your leads material, property listings, and customized communications by utilizing the data that is kept in your CRM. This customization greatly raises the likelihood of conversion while also demonstrating your dedication to their particular demands. Leads are more inclined to interact with you when you provide them with information that fits with their interests and preferences.

3. Take the Lead:

Establishing Trust Through Time
Not every lead is prepared to convert immediately. It could take some time for them to consider their options and develop confidence in your services. CRM makes lead nurturing possible, which is the practice of maintaining contact with leads

over time and ensuring that they remember your brand and level of competence. Follow-up plans and automated reminders make sure that no lead is overlooked.

4. Effective Communication:
Simplifying Your Process.
Timely communication is crucial in the real estate industry because things move quickly. CRM solutions make your workflow more efficient by automatically answering questions, reminding you to follow up, and making sure that no correspondence is missed. In addition to saving you time, this effective communication gives your leads the impression that you are a knowledgeable and approachable real estate agent.

5. Data-Informed Decision-Making:
Enhancing Your Approach

The information kept in your CRM is meant for analysis as well as reference. You may learn a lot about lead behavior, the success of your marketing campaigns, and opportunities for development by evaluating the data gathered. You can make well-informed decisions and modify your strategy to suit the changing needs of your leads with this data-driven approach.

6. Monitoring Conversion Progress:
Seeing Achievement

CRM systems come equipped with tools for following your leads as they move through the sales funnel. Which leads are in the awareness, interest, contemplation, or intent stages may be seen with ease. By concentrating on leads with the highest conversion rates, you can use this data to better efficiently manage your time and resources.

7. Retention & Referrals:

Going Beyond Sales

CRM has advantages that go beyond conversion. They can assist you in maintaining current client ties by sending birthday, anniversary, and property anniversaries reminders. Client satisfaction can lead to brand ambassadors and reference sources, which can be a great way for your real estate company to develop.

CRM becomes the cornerstone of your plan as you work to assemble a seven-figure real estate team. It simplifies your procedures, adds personality to your strategy, and gives you the ability to turn more leads into devoted customers. You may take your real estate company to new heights and achieve the highest level of success in this fast-paced sector by utilizing CRM.

Part IV:

Scaling Your Team and Business

Chapter 7: Expanding Your Team

The Growth Catalyst for Your Real Estate Empire

One thing becomes very evident in the unrelenting chase of a 7-figure real estate team and business: scaling up is necessary for success. In order to pull off something as incredible as this, you have to be constantly assessing your operations' latent development and potential for expansion. Building a successful real estate empire takes strategy, creativity, and most importantly, being prepared to grow your staff. Now, let's explore this crucial facet of growing your company.

Imagine the story of Sarah, a real estate agent who started off as a lone agent. Her clientele developed steadily as a result of her commitment and diligence. But as her clients' expectations grew, she discovered herself juggling a lot of different obligations.

Although it was a success story, there were difficulties along the way. She knew she was wasting time, that she was passing up opportunities to do business. It was then that she realized how important it was to grow her staff.

The following explains why growing your staff is a crucial step towards building a seven-figure real estate business:

1. Multitasking To Mastery:

As a lone agent, your skills are spread across multiple responsibilities, such as client consultations, advertising, record-keeping, and bargaining. You can focus your knowledge on what you do best by growing your staff. Every team member can flourish in their own duties and add to the general prosperity of your company.

2. Additional Bandwidth:

Growing your team gives you additional capacity to serve a wider range of customers. You can serve more clients if your team consists of a larger number of people. This increases your earning potential and strengthens your reputation as a responsive and dependable person.

3. Diversity of Skill Sets:

A larger team has members with a wider range of skill sets. People who excel in areas where you may be weak can be hired. Your team may handle every aspect of marketing, technology, and negotiation, guaranteeing thorough client care.

4. Continuity and Growth:

Your company can maintain continuity if its personnel are well-organized. The team's activities don't stop even if one member takes a break or leaves. Growth depends on this stability since it allows you to concentrate on long-term plans while leaving day-to-day duties to competent people.

5. Unleashing Innovation:
Growing your workforce brings in new ideas and viewpoints. As a solo agent, you might not have thought of some of the creative techniques and strategies that other team members can offer. In the highly competitive real estate market, this may be revolutionary.

6. Leveraging Expertise:
You may benefit from the expertise and experience of experts when you include them on your team. Their ideas, whether they come from legal, financial, or technological knowledge, can protect your company and improve the quality of your services.

Sarah's story demonstrates how her real estate practice was altered by her decision to grow her staff. She was able to concentrate on her love of building relationships with clients and property appraisal by hiring a buyer's agent, a transaction coordinator, and a marketing specialist. Her firm reached new heights as a result of this development, and she eventually achieved her goal of building a seven-figure real estate team.

Growing your workforce is not just an option—it's a requirement as you embark on the incredible path of scaling your real estate company. The tale of Sarah shows that you are creating more than simply a company when you leverage the abilities of a diverse and talented staff. You are creating a legacy. Your seven-figure real estate team is well within your reach with the proper personnel at your side, and your real estate career path is nothing short of extraordinary.

Furthermore, keep in mind that team growth is the key to your success as you begin the process of scaling your real estate team. By doing this, you're creating a legacy as well as a business. Your path to the top of a seven-figure real estate business is a diverse, talented workforce.

Your path to real estate success may be a wonderful one filled with development, efficiency, and strategic excellence if you have the proper person at your side.

Expanding Your List of Agents Increasing the Number of Agents on Your Team: Building a Scalable Real Estate Team.

Growing your team is a crucial step towards scalability and success if you want to develop a seven-figure real estate team. Without adding too much drama, let's discuss the strategic relevance of expanding your agent roster and how it might affect your real estate business's future.

1. Increased Client Servicing Capability: The capacity to serve a wider clientele is one of the main benefits of growing your staff. You can effectively and efficiently handle a larger volume of clients by expanding your agent roster. This increases your earning potential as well as your reputation for providing top-notch services.

2. Make Use of Specialized Knowledge:
Expanding your group enables you to add agents with specific knowledge. People that are exceptional in particular fields, such investment properties, commercial real estate, or luxury properties, can be hired. Your ability to offer a wide range of clients full service is ensured by this diversity.

3. Geographic Expansion:
As your team grows, you may want to think about extending your reach

geographically. By having agents cover various regions, communities, or even entire cities, you may expand the reach of your company by taking advantage of new markets and opportunities.

4. Enhanced Productivity and Efficiency: You may assign duties and responsibilities more effectively when your team is larger. You may streamline processes and increase productivity and customer service efficiency by having each team member concentrate on their specific area of expertise.

5. Improved Lead Generation and Marketing:

More agents on the roster equates to more people actively engaged in lead generation and marketing. This broadens your prospect pool by increasing your reach and your capacity to draw in new customers.

6. Risk Mitigation:

Several agents can share the risks involved in real estate transactions when the team is larger. This method of risk reduction offers stability and protects your company from unforeseen difficulties.

7. Succession Planning:

As your real estate company expands, you'll need to think about how to maintain operations over the long run. You can put in place a succession plan by adding more agents to your roster, which will facilitate a seamless transition in the event that important team members choose to retire or take on new challenges.

8. Creating a Recognizable Brand:

As more agents represent your team, the market will see a greater visibility and recognition of your brand. More customer recommendations, recognition, and trust may result from this enhanced visibility. In conclusion, expanding your agent network is a wise strategic choice that can help you grow your real estate company in many ways. It broadens your geographic reach, boosts operational efficiency, increases your capacity to service clients, and makes use of specialized knowledge.

As you work to develop a seven-figure real estate team, keep in mind that expanding your agent base is essential to your success and scalability. It's a deliberate move that will help your company flourish and establish you as the real estate industry leader.

Employing Help Personnel
Adding Support Workers to Your Real Estate Team to Achieve Scalable Success.

Hiring support workers to increase your team is one of the most important stages toward scalability and success in your goal to develop a 7-figure real estate business. This is a critical strategic step that will impact how your real estate firm develops in the future. We won't add a tale here, but let's talk about why recruiting support workers is critical to reaching your scaling goals.

1. Administrative Efficiency:

You can significantly increase your team's administrative efficiency by hiring support personnel including transaction coordinators, administrative assistants, and office managers. Real estate agents can concentrate on their primary duties of serving customers and closing deals by delegating paperwork, scheduling, and everyday operating activities to these experts.

2. Improved Customer Service:

Support employees are essential to your team's ability to provide excellent customer service. They are able to handle customer inquiries, give updates, and guarantee effective communication. Increased customer satisfaction and retention can result from providing excellent customer service.

3. Time Management:

Your time is important as the leader of a real estate team. Employing support personnel enables you to assign labor-intensive duties, allowing you to focus on strategy, customer acquisition, and business expansion. This effective time management has a major role in your success as a whole.

4. Expertise in Niche Functions:

Support employees may contribute their knowledge of specific fields like data analysis, social media management, and marketing. Your company can gain a lot from these niche functions by enhancing marketing initiatives, producing leads, and offering insightful market data.

5. Streamlined Operations:

Your team can simplify everyday tasks with the help of knowledgeable support personnel. Better coordination, more effective transaction management, and increased capacity to handle more clients and properties are the outcomes of this streamlining.

6. Business Expansion and Diversification:

Your team can concentrate on strategic expansion projects by hiring support people. You may grow into new markets, diversify your services, and look into new business opportunities when administrative and operational responsibilities are handled effectively.

7. Stress Reduction:

Support personnel help real estate agents by reducing their burden and stress. A more productive team, better job satisfaction, and a healthier work atmosphere are all correlated with lower stress levels.

8. Business Scalability:

Hiring support people is crucial to growing your operations as your team grows. These experts are essential to preserving consistency and high standards of service even as your company grows.

To sum up, recruiting support personnel is an essential first step toward growing your real estate team and attaining scalable success. It improves customer service, boosts administrative effectiveness, and has time management advantages. Support workers expedite processes, promote corporate growth and diversity, and add specific experience to your team. It also sets up your team for scalability and is essential for reducing stress.

Understanding the value of recruiting support workers is essential to your success and business growth as you strive to build a seven-figure real estate team.

**Education and Training
Developing a 7-Figure Real Estate Team
via Training.**

Training and development play a crucial part when you set out to grow your real estate team and business to a seven-figure income. A high-achieving team that continuously produces outstanding outcomes depends on the caliber of training and opportunity for continued development.

We will discuss the importance of these elements and how they support the development and success of your team, even though there may not be a narrative here.

1. Knowledge Enhancement:

Developing your team's knowledge base is made possible through training and development. By giving your agents and support personnel access to the most recent market trends, legal updates, and industry best practices, you provide them the tools they need to succeed in their positions.

2. Skill Refinement:

Those in the real estate industry need to keep improving their abilities. Through training programs, your team can improve their sales, communication, and negotiation abilities. In a dynamic market, this ongoing improvement guarantees that your staff stays productive and competitive.

3. Consistency in Service:

Providing consistent service is essential to obtaining and preserving a seven-figure status. Training ensures that everyone on the team has the same perspective on managing properties, interacting with clients, and acting ethically, which results in reliable and superior service.

4. Adaptation to Technology:

As technology advances, the real estate sector also changes. Through training, your staff may stay technologically adept by adjusting to new tools and processes. Maintaining an advantage over competitors and running effective operations depend on this adaptation.

5. Professional Development:
The individual and professional development of your team members are strongly related. Offering chances for industry designations, certifications, and skill-specific training improves their knowledge while also boosting motivation and morale.

6. Increased Retention of Staff:
Investing in training and development shows that you care about the success of your staff. This dedication can result in much higher employee retention rates, lower turnover expenses, and a more dependable, competent team.

7. Flexibility in Response to Market Shifts:

The real estate market is prone to swings. Training gives your team the flexibility it needs to take advantage of opportunities, adjust to changes in the market, and successfully overcome obstacles.

8. Enhanced Leadership:

As your team expands, it's critical that individual members acquire leadership abilities. Training courses on management, teamwork, and leadership can assist in laying a solid basis for leadership in your company.

9. Brand Reputation:

The reputation of your company is enhanced when a well-trained staff continuously produces excellent outcomes. When your staff is regarded for its professionalism and expertise, clients and partners are more likely to trust you and suggest your services.

10. Competitive Edge:

Lastly, a major competitive edge is provided by the education and growth of your real estate workforce. A committed, experienced, and well-versed staff is more likely to surpass rivals and reach seven-figure success.

Developing your team through training and development is essential to improving their knowledge, abilities, and consistency while building a 7-figure real estate team. It guarantees flexibility in response to technological advancements and shifts in the market, helps retain employees, and strengthens the leadership qualities within your team.

In the end, putting a strong emphasis on training and development sets up your real estate team for long-term success and scalability in a cutthroat market.

Chapter 8.

Scaling Your Operations

Scaling Your Operations: The Key to 7-Figure Success

Picture a busy real estate office with clients coming in by the hour, phones ringing nonstop, and deals concluding one after the other. When aiming for seven figures of achievement, this is the objective that every aspirational real estate agent has in mind. But growing your operations is crucial if you want to make this ambition a reality.

Let's examine the reasons why scaling is important, and we'll add a narrative to highlight the point.

A sudden increase in client inquiries once overwhelmed Sarah, a committed real estate representative in a modest real estate company. Her reputation for providing flawless service had taken off, resulting in an influx of enquiries. She was ecstatic at first, but soon found that she was unable to manage things on her own. Clients were starting to sense the stress as calls were missing and paperwork was mounting.

The Importance of Scaling.

More than merely allowing for growth, scaling your operations is making sure your company keeps running smoothly and effectively even as it grows.
This is why it's so important:

1.Managing an Expanding Workload:
As your company expands, so does the amount of work it produces. By scaling your operations, you can make sure that your staff can manage more customers, transactions, and work without sacrificing quality.

2. Better Customer Experience:
In Sarah's instance, scalability would have ensured that each customer got the same degree of care and support. Clients still receive the same level of commitment and professionalism even when operations are scaled back.

3. Efficient Workflow:
Workflow is streamlined by a thoughtful scaling strategy. This makes things easier for your team and your clients by

minimizing errors, avoiding missed opportunities, and reducing bottlenecks.

4. Financial Sustainability:

Scaling involves sustaining profitability as well as growing sales. Effective operations ensure long-term financial sustainability by avoiding wasteful spending and resource waste.

5. Team Empowerment:

Burnout and low morale can result from an overworked team. By growing your operations, you may enable your workforce to flourish instead of merely endure, which creates a happier workplace.

Going back to our narrative, Sarah saw that scaling was necessary. She put effective CRM software in place to handle customer interactions, hired an assistant to help with administrative duties, and created clear procedures to guarantee that each and every client received the same high caliber of care. As a result, her company expanded in addition to being able to handle the increase in customers.

6. Growth Potential:

Scalability makes room for additional development. It offers the groundwork for entering new markets, looking into new services, or growing internationally.

7. Brand Reputation:

Maintaining a great reputation for your brand requires consistently providing high-quality service, especially during times of fast expansion. Whether you own a major real estate company or a tiny boutique firm, your clients know they can rely on you.

The link between your current performance and seven-figure wealth is scaling your activities. It guarantees that your company can effectively manage expansion, uphold a high standard of service, and provide the groundwork for sustained success. Sarah's example shows that even small agencies can succeed in the face of quick success if they understand when scaling is necessary and put the correct tactics in place.

Effective Growth Management
**Effective Growth Management: A Key
to Scaling Your Business**

Reaching a seven-figure income in real estate is a noteworthy achievement. But reaching this degree of affluence requires a carefully considered plan for efficiently controlling expansion. Rapid expansion can cause turmoil and lower the level of service you offer your customers if it is not managed properly. In this section, we'll go over the fundamentals of successfully managing growth when scaling your business.

1. Strategic Planning:

Having a well-defined plan in place is essential for managing growth. Setting objectives, identifying required resources, and delineating a methodical plan of action are all part of strategic planning. Planning should cover a range of topics, including operational, marketing, and financial strategies.

2. Technology Investing:

As your real estate company expands, you'll need to make investments in software and hardware that can automate and streamline operations. To increase productivity and uphold service quality, this comprises project management instruments, communication platforms, and customer relationship management (CRM) systems.

3. Scalable Procedures:

For reliable and effective operations, scalable procedures must be developed. When your company grows, new team members should be able to quickly become familiar with your systems by following standard operating procedures, documenting your workflows, and identifying areas that can be automated.

4. Team Development:

Building your team to meet the demands of your growing company is essential to effective growth management. As your business expands, empower your staff to take on increasingly important duties by investing in their education and training.

5. Financial Management:

As your firm grows, managing your funds gets more difficult. Make budgets, keep an eye on your cash flow, and periodically evaluate your financial situation. This will assist you in making prudent resource allocations and getting ready for unforeseen obstacles.

6. Client-Centric Approach:

It's imperative to keep your approach client-centric as you expand. Make sure each customer continues to receive exceptional service and individualized attention. This entails establishing unambiguous channels of communication and upholding service standards.

7. Quality Control:

Consistent quality control is necessary for growth management to be effective. Establish procedures for inspecting and assessing your offerings to make sure that customers are given the greatest possible experience and that your brand's reputation is upheld.

8. Market Research:

Keep up with industry developments and carry out further market research. With this information, you'll be able to change with the times and stay ahead of the competition in the real estate market.

9. Scaling Responsibly:

Development must be sustainable and conscientious. Steer clear of expanding quickly without the required infrastructure and resources. Review each stage of your expansion plan and make any necessary corrections.

10. Adaptability:

Lastly, have an open mind and be flexible. In the real estate industry, adaptability is crucial, and your growth plan should change as the market and your clients' requirements do.

In conclusion, scaling your operations to develop a seven-figure real estate team requires good growth management. It guarantees that your company can continue to provide the same level of service, adjust to rising demand, and prosper in a cutthroat industry. You can continue to pursue greatness and achieve new levels of achievement by following these guidelines.

**Developing Scalable Frameworks.
Developing Scalable Systems: The
Secret to Effective Expansion.**

It's admirable to want to grow your real
estate team and scale your operations, but
doing so effectively calls for putting
scalable procedures in place. A key idea in
business is scalability, which guarantees
that your company can expand without
sacrificing consistency and efficiency.

Here, we'll discuss how crucial it is to
develop scalable mechanisms in order to
develop a seven-figure real estate team.

1. Effective Workflow Architecture:
It starts with a well-designed workflow to
create a scalable system. Think about all
of the many jobs and procedures that go
into running your real estate business,

from generating leads to onboarding clients and finalizing deals. Every step needs to be well recorded and efficiently optimized.

2. Automation and Technology Integration:

Scalability requires technology utilization. Invest in solutions that can automate repetitive work and streamline processes, such as customer relationship management (CRM) systems and real estate software. Your staff will be able to concentrate on high-value tasks while saving time and reducing errors thanks to this.

3. Standardization of Processes:

Provide your staff with established protocols and processes to adhere to. By doing this, it's made sure that everyone understands the system and can quickly adjust to it. Additionally, standardization improves the caliber of your offerings and streamlines the onboarding process for new employees as your company grows.

4. Clear Channels of Communication: Scalability requires effective communication. Establish clear lines of communication with clients and within your staff. Assuring prompt responses, establishing expectations, and upholding transparency are all part of this real estate transaction.

5. Resource Allocation: You can more efficiently distribute resources when your system is scalable. This entails financial planning and budgeting in addition to overseeing the time and effort of your team. Make sure you have the resources needed to back up your expansion plans.

6. Scalable Lead Generation and Marketing:

As your company grows, your lead generation and marketing plans should be flexible enough to meet the escalating demand. This entails using digital marketing, varying your marketing channels, and developing a lead generation and nurturing plan.

7. Quality Control and Feedback:

Quality does not have to be sacrificed for scalability. Implement systems for gathering customer feedback and quality control procedures. This will assist you in maintaining a high degree of customer satisfaction and helping you to continuously enhance your services.

8. Team Development and Training:
Make an investment in your team's growth
and education. Your team members should
develop the abilities and know-how
necessary to take on additional tasks as
your business expands. This guarantees
that your group can adjust to the needs of
a bigger company.

**9. Data Analytics and Performance
Metrics:**
Track the effectiveness of your scalable
systems with the help of data analytics and
key performance indicators (KPIs). Assess
and review your operations on a regular
basis to make data-driven improvements.

10. Scalable Growth plan:
A scalable growth plan is necessary for a
scaling process to be successful. Establish
precise objectives, due dates, and

benchmarks for your growth. Be ready to modify your plan as your company grows to satisfy consumer needs.

Developing scalable systems is a continuous process that enables your real estate team to expand and thrive without sacrificing effectiveness or level of service. It's a calculated method that puts your company in the best possible position for sustained success and gives you the ability to become a seven-figure real estate team leader.

Planning and Budgeting for Finances. Budgeting and Financial Planning are the Cornerstones of Growing Your Real Estate Company.

Strong financial planning and budgeting are essential if you want to grow your real estate team and business to the coveted seven-figure level. These two essential elements form the cornerstone for effectively and ethically overseeing your business operations as your real estate empire grows.

Here, we go into detail about how crucial budgeting and financial planning are to your efforts to create a profitable seven-figure real estate company.

1. Strategic Growth:

The cornerstone of strategic growth is financial planning. It entails establishing precise financial objectives, deadlines, and a plan for achieving them. You can make wise choices about growing your workforce, purchasing technology, and obtaining resources if you have a clear plan in place.

2. Resource Allocation:

Budgeting guarantees the proper distribution of your resources. You can allocate money for necessary expenditures like marketing, technology improvements, staff pay, and overhead by making a thorough budget. Allocating resources wisely keeps you from going over budget and aids in keeping your cash flow positive.

3. Risk Mitigation:

Like any industry, real estate has its share of inherent dangers. You can identify possible hazards and create strategies for mitigating them with the help of financial planning. This could entail setting up backup plans in case of revenue volatility or constructing a financial cushion to cover unforeseen costs.

4. Investment Decisions:

As you develop, you'll come across a range of options and possibilities for investments. Planning your finances gives you the tools to carefully consider these choices. Is it time to enter a new market? Is it the right moment to make a real estate technology investment? You can accelerate your progress by making well-informed decisions that are in line with your financial plan.

5. Performance Tracking:

Budgeting and financial planning provide a clear window into the productivity of your real estate staff. By keeping a regular eye on your financial data, you can pinpoint areas that are working well and those that could use improvement. Metrics and KPI tracking allows you to assess how well your operations are working.

6. Adaptable Strategy:

Your financial planning needs to change as your company and staff grow. Be ready to modify your financial plan in response to unforeseen obstacles and new opportunities. Being nimble is essential for sustained success.

7. Financial Control:

Budgeting and financial planning provide you a degree of control over your finances that is essential for stability and expansion. With a thorough understanding of your earnings and outlays, you'll be able to make decisions in real time to improve your financial situation.

8. Scaling Responsibly:

Reaching seven figures requires responsible growth. You won't overstretch your resources when expanding thanks to your financial plan. It helps you avoid financial strain by advising you on the best time and rate of expansion.

9. Cash Flow Management:

Cash flow management is supported by good budgeting. The stability and reputation of your real estate company depend on your capacity to pay for ongoing costs, initiate new projects, and pay bills on schedule.

10. Long-Term Sustainability:
In the end, your seven-figure real estate team's long-term viability is influenced by prudent financial planning and budgeting. They support you while you handle market swings, negotiate business obstacles, and grasp expansion prospects.

By including budgeting and financial planning into your business strategy, you create a solid financial base that helps your real estate team expand and leads to the esteemed seven-figure mark. By fostering self-control, responsibility, and adaptability, these techniques guarantee a financially safe and fulfilling path.

Part V: Thriving in a Competitive Market

Chapter 9: Navigating Market Challenges.

Navigating Market Challenges: Thriving in a Competitive Real Estate Landscape

A seven-figure real estate team's capacity to overcome market obstacles is a distinguishing feature in the real estate industry, where possibilities abound and competition is intense. The path to creating a successful company must involve tactics for prospering in a fiercely competitive market. Let me tell you a story to help you understand the significance of this endeavor:

Two real estate teams set out on their mission for success right in the middle of a busy city. Despite their early successes, Team A chose to relax and be satisfied with their present tactics. But Team B, under the direction of a visionary leader, realized they had to change to meet changing market conditions.

The landscape of real estate changed over time. As more firms entered the market and technology changed how real estate was purchased and sold, the competition in the market grew. Team A encountered difficulties obtaining leads, keeping clients, and being current. Their commercial position gradually deteriorated as a result of their unwillingness to adjust.

Conversely, Team B welcomed change. They embraced cutting-edge technology to improve their web presence, expedite business processes, and deliver top-notch customer service. They carefully sought out market trends and modified their plans in response. They continued to draw in business and uphold their reputation as a seven-figure real estate team as a consequence.

Team A struggled during economic downturns because they were unable to handle the choppy waters of market difficulties. On the other hand, Team B had developed financial resilience by astute budgeting and financial planning. They were ready for even more success when the market recovered after they had withstood economic storms.

As the narrative progressed, Team A became aware of the mistake of their complacency. They recognized the importance of adaptability and aggressive strategies in the ever-changing real estate industry. They started expanding their service offerings, improving their marketing approaches, and implementing technical breakthroughs. They needed some time to get back on track, but their redoubled efforts were fruitful.

Both teams eventually had to deal with market obstacles. But Team B's determination to meet these obstacles head-on and their calculated strategy let them succeed in a cutthroat industry, hitting the seven-figure threshold that Team A could only dream of.
This narrative emphasizes the important lesson: You have to be open to change,

take proactive measures to overcome obstacles, and continuously adjust to market dynamics if you want to succeed in a cutthroat real estate market and develop a seven-figure team. Being able to keep ahead of the curve in the ever-changing real estate market is essential for long-term success.

Overcoming market obstacles is about more than just surviving; it's about realizing your real estate goals and leaving a lasting legacy. Your route to a seven-figure real estate team becomes not just achievable but also a worthwhile endeavor by researching market trends, putting creative methods into practice, and maintaining an open mind.

Furthermore, being able to successfully navigate market hurdles is essential to

surviving as a seven-figure team in the fast-paced world of real estate. Long-term success depends on your ability to adapt to and prosper in a competitive market, which can present both opportunities and challenges.
Here, we'll look at the tactics and factors that need to be taken into account in order to succeed in the cutthroat real estate market.

1. Market Research and Analysis:
Thorough research and analysis are essential for success in a cutthroat market. Making educated selections will be aided by your knowledge of regional and local market trends, demography, and economic indicators. By focusing on the appropriate locations and properties, you can increase your chances of success with this knowledge.

2. Technological Developments:
Adopting technology is now required; it is
no longer discretionary. Make use of
cutting-edge tools and technologies to stay
ahead of the curve. Online marketing
platforms, property management software,
and customer relationship management
(CRM) systems are examples of this.
Technology improves your capacity to
communicate with clients while also
streamlining operations.

3. Online Presence:
Having a strong online presence is
essential in the current digital era.
Professional, educational, and captivating
content should be featured on your
website, social media accounts, and online
advertisements. Developing a strong
online brand aids in credibility building
and client attraction.

4. Diversified Services:

You can differentiate yourself from the competition by providing a range of real estate services. Think about branching out into real estate investing, property management, or other specialized markets that fit the qualifications and experience of your group. By diversifying, you can increase your market share.

5. Financial Resilience:

Make sure you budget and plan wisely to be ready for economic downturns. You can weather market swings, take advantage of investment possibilities, and contribute to the development of your team by keeping your financial profile in good shape.

6. Networking and Partnerships:

It's imperative to establish a network of useful contacts within the real estate sector. Work together with contractors, mortgage brokers, and other experts to offer your clients complete services. Referrals are another benefit of networking; these can be a big source of new business.

7. Adaptability and Innovation:

Allow yourself to modify your plans in response to feedback from the market. One characteristic that distinguishes high-achieving teams is their capacity to change course and introduce new ideas when needed. Gaining a competitive edge may require keeping an eye on your rivals and remaining adaptable.

8. Client-Centric Approach:

What sets us apart is our exceptional client service. Make sure everyone on your team is dedicated to providing top-notch service from the first point of contact to the point of closure. Contented customers bring in repeat business and recommendations, which are essential to your company's expansion.

9. Marketing and Branding:

Create a strong marketing plan that is specific to your intended market. Both offline and online initiatives are included in this. Your branding should distinguish you in a crowded market by expressing trust, knowledge, and dependability.

10. Education and Training:

Make an investment in your team's ongoing education and training. It's critical to keep up with industry developments and legal requirements. When it comes to handling customer demands and market difficulties, well-trained agents perform better.

In conclusion, developing a seven-figure team and succeeding in a cutthroat real estate market necessitate a multifaceted strategy. Accept technology, broaden your offerings, and continue to be flexible. Your ability to overcome obstacles in the industry and give your customers outstanding service will determine how successful you are. You may use change and staying ahead of market trends to transform a competitive environment into a foundation for success and growth.

**Changing with the Market.
A Strategic Approach to Achieving
Success in a Competitive Real Estate
Market: Adjusting to Market Changes**

Developing a 7-figure real estate team in the dynamic world of real estate requires the ability to adjust to changes in the market. Success or stagnation may depend on one's capacity to identify and react to shifts in the market. In this section, we'll look at how to adjust to market changes so that your team can keep growing and succeeding.

1. Constant Monitoring:

Keeping a close check on local, regional, and national real estate trends is one of the first steps in adjusting to market changes. This involves monitoring shifts in customer preferences, interest rates, inventory levels, and property values. Making educated decisions starts with staying informed.

2. Data Analytics: Data is the most useful instrument you have to adjust to changes in the market. You can spot trends and predict changes in the market by analyzing both historical and present data. Make data-driven decisions by utilizing economic indicators, market analysis tools, and customer relationship management (CRM) systems.

3. Pricing Flexibility: In a cutthroat industry, price can be a major success factor. Be ready to modify listing prices in response to changes in the market. Even in a changing market, a home with a competitive pricing is more likely to draw in buyers and expedite sales.

4. Specialized Niches:

Take into account focusing on specialist markets that can be less impacted by changes in the overall market. These might be upscale homes, business real estate, or exclusive neighborhoods. The impact of market swings might be lessened by diversifying your area of expertise.

5. Property Management:

Even in difficult sales markets, diversifying into property management can offer a steady source of income. Your revenue can be stabilized during market downturns with the support of rental income.

6. Marketing and Branding Plan:

You should have a flexible marketing and branding plan. Adjust your messaging to reflect the state of the market. Emphasize the advantages of purchasing or selling in the current market conditions, and back up your arguments with facts.

7. Financial Prudence:

To withstand changes in the market, keep a strong financial base. Create cash reserves that will help your team through times of adversity. Investment strategies, savings plans, and budgeting should all be part of a solid financial plan.

8. Innovation and Agility:

Be able to change course when called for. To succeed in a market that is highly competitive, one needs to be innovative and agile. To adapt to changing customer needs, seize new possibilities, adopt cutting-edge technologies, and create innovative solutions.

9. Client-Centric Approach:

A consistent approach is to concentrate on providing outstanding client service. Content customers are more likely to stick with you and recommend you to others, which will keep your firm afloat when the market changes.

10. Real-Time Communication:

It's critical to have open and honest communication with clients. Give them regular updates on the state of the market and explain how these could affect their decisions to buy or sell. You may improve your reputation and create enduring client relationships by being a reliable source of information.

In conclusion, a key component of succeeding in a cutthroat real estate market is being able to adjust to changes in the market. Building a seven-figure real estate team that can withstand market swings and keep expanding requires this flexibility. You may capitalize on changes in the industry by being well-informed, utilizing data to guide decisions, and adapting your tactics. Recall that being flexible is a deliberate approach to long-term success in the real estate sector, not merely a reaction to change.

**Managing Economic Recessions.
Managing Economic Downturns: An
Adaptable Strategy for Succeeding in a
Cutthroat Real Estate Market.**

Similar to other industries, the real estate sector is not impervious to economic downturns. Top real estate teams distinguish themselves by their ability to navigate through difficult times, whether they are brought on by regional issues or general economic situations. This section will cover tactics for managing recessions so that your seven-figure real estate team may keep expanding and succeeding.

1. Diversification of Services:

You should think about broadening your offerings while the economy is struggling. Offering property management, relocation services, and real estate investing in addition to standard buying and selling can generate additional income.

2. Invest in Training:

Make the most of downturns to propel your team's professional development. To increase your knowledge and bring your clients greater value, spend money on education and training.

3. Cost Control:

Keep a close eye on the spending of your group. Reassess and cut non-essential expenses to keep profits high. This entails determining your operating costs, workplace space requirements, and marketing budget.

4. Investigate original financing options:

For your clients by following this link. Getting funding during recessions can be difficult. Deals can be closed more quickly if one is knowledgeable about several financing choices, such as seller financing or government-backed loans.

5. Focus On Specialist Markets:

That might be more robust to downturns in the economy. For example, properties in retirement communities, historic areas, or certain neighborhoods could hold their value better in hard times.

6. Pricing Strategies:

Modify your pricing tactics as necessary. Even during a slump, correct pricing may guarantee that your homes sell swiftly. Stay adaptable and take into account competitive pricing without sacrificing profitability.

7. **Marketing that Works:**

Boost your advertising tactics. By concentrating on focused, economical digital marketing, your team may remain visible and draw in prospective investors or customers.

8. **Client Communication:**

During economic downturns, it is essential to have regular and transparent communication with clients. Providing reassurance and up-to-date market knowledge helps foster trust and loyalty among clients who may be more wary.

9. **Property Evaluation:**

The caliber of the properties you represent becomes critical during a downturn. In difficult market conditions, carefully assess and choose properties that are likely to hold or improve in value.

10. Financial Reserves:
Set up and keep funds aside for emergencies. During recessions, having a safety net can help your business weather the storm. Establish reserves to pay for operating expenses when revenue is low.

11. Comprehensive Market Research:
This is essential. Making decisions can be aided by having a thorough understanding of the supply and demand, foreclosure rates, and historical trends of your local market.

12. Legal and Compliance Expertise:
Keep abreast on legal and compliance matters, especially those that come up during recessions. These could include government initiatives that could affect your clients or rules pertaining to short sales or foreclosures.

Your seven-figure real estate team may weather economic downturns with resilience and maintain its success in a cutthroat real estate market by taking proactive measures to address these problems. There will be difficulties, but there may also be chances for development and creativity. Regardless of the state of the economy, you can maintain your team's position as an industry leader by adapting and responding with effectiveness.

Remaining Ahead of the Contest. Keeping Up with the Competition: Gaining an Advantage in a Difficult Real Estate Market

Being successful in a cutthroat real estate market is no easy task, particularly in hard times financially. You need to continuously outperform the competition in addition to being able to adjust to changes in the market if you want to develop a seven-figure real estate team. The following are crucial tactics to make sure your team continues to succeed and you keep one step ahead of the competition:

1. Superb Customer Service:
Providing excellent customer service ought to be a given. Going above and above for your customers builds a solid

reputation that encourages recommendations and recurring business.

2. Leveraging Technology:
Make use of the newest tools and technologies available for real estate. To improve your service and draw in tech-savvy customers, make use of technologies like virtual tours, social media marketing, customer relationship management (CRM) systems, and others.

3. Comprehensive Market Knowledge:
Keep abreast of regional and national market situations. Customers appreciate agents who can offer them insightful analysis and data-driven recommendations.

4. Networking:

Create and maintain connections within your neighborhood real estate market. Networking can offer chances for cooperation, recommendations, and useful industry knowledge.

5. Specialization:

Take into consideration specializing in a certain area of the real estate industry, such as eco-friendly homes, luxury residences, or commercial real estate. Having a specialty might help you stand out and draw in clients who are looking for knowledge.

6. All-encompassing Marketing:

Create a comprehensive marketing plan that incorporates traditional and digital techniques. This covers email marketing, social media, content marketing, search engine optimization (SEO), and even print advertising.

7. Client-Centric Approach:

Customize your offerings to meet the specific requirements and tastes of your customers. By putting the needs of your clients first, you may increase client satisfaction and establish yourself as a reliable real estate expert.

8. Team Development:

Make constant investments in the advancement of your group. Providing training, coaching, and assistance may guarantee that your agents remain at the top of their game and continue to provide exceptional service.

9. Community Development:
Get involved in the community by volunteering, sponsoring events, and joining groups in your neighborhood. Engagement in the community that is constructive can boost trust and brand reputation.

10. Effective Communication:
It's essential to communicate. Establish a smooth and reliable connection by listening to your clients' issues, answering their questions in a timely manner, and communicating openly.

11. Online Testimonials and Reviews:
Invite happy customers to post testimonials and reviews online. Good feedback on sites like Google, Yelp, and Zillow can improve your reputation and foster trust among prospective customers.

12. Constant Learning:

Make an investment in your own learning and development. To make sure you're offering the finest service possible, keep up with the latest developments in the real estate market, best practices, and laws.

13. Adaptability:

Be flexible and receptive to novel approaches and concepts. The real estate industry is always changing, and those who can adjust fast tend to have an advantage.

By applying these tactics on a regular basis, your seven-figure real estate team will be able to maintain its leadership position in your community as well as its competitiveness. Recall that striving for greatness is an ongoing process. You can create a successful real estate company by

being committed to innovation and
keeping your attention on the needs of
your clients.

Chapter 10. Achieving Long-Term Success

Attaining Long-Term Success: Maintaining Quality in a Cutthroat Real Estate Industry.

In the real estate industry, where conditions can be unstable and competition intense, long-term success is a desired but difficult objective. Embracing a long-term view is critical to building a seven-figure real estate team that not only survives but thrives in such an environment. Let's examine how a success story of tenacity, flexibility, and unrelenting dedication to quality might direct your own path.

A long time ago, in the thriving metropolis of Metroville, two real estate firms named Team A and Team B set out to dominate the cutthroat industry. Both teams were ready to leave their imprint, had a wealth of expertise, and were well-equipped. Their methods were very different from one another, though.

Team A: Immediate Success and Temporary Benefits
Team A was committed to having an effect right away. They frequently put numbers before quality, concentrating on speedy deals and rapid gains. Their agents had a reputation for closing deals quickly, and they undoubtedly made a sizable sum of money quickly.

However, as the months stretched into years, Team A noticed a pattern.

Numerous patrons expressed dissatisfaction with the expedited procedure and believed that their distinct requirements were disregarded. Referrals and repeat business began to decline as the number of negative internet reviews increased.

The Long-Term Visionaries make up Team B.

Conversely, Team B took a long-term strategy. They understood that each real estate deal was more than simply a purchase; it was a chance to establish rapport, foster confidence, and deliver first-rate service. They made investments in their agents' career advancement, fostering knowledge and a profound comprehension of the unique needs of each of their clients.

Initially, individuals who preferred immediate outcomes were skeptical of Team B's strategy since it appeared more deliberate. But their dedication to quality work and client satisfaction started to pay off. Clients who were happy spoke highly about the staff and became ardent supporters.

The Shifting Moment

A turning point occurred during a period of economic decline. Both teams faced uncertainty when the real estate market crashed. While Team B persisted in their dedication to long-term success, Team A faltered in their attempt to restore their quick transaction pace.

A Targeted Reverse

Team B quickly adjusted to the change in the market. They used technology to improve their remote services and reached out to the community, offering insightful information on the market's comeback. Their clientele had faith in them to handle the chaos.

After realizing the shortcomings of their quick-hit plan, Team A changed course, motivated by Team B's accomplishments. Taking a cue from the long-term visionaries, they too started concentrating on developing solid client connections.

The Fallout

With time, Team B not only made it through the competitive market, but also prospered there. They kept up a fantastic reputation and experienced a sharp increase in referrals and repeat business. Even though Team A was able to bounce back and restore their reputation, they understood the value of taking a long-term strategy.

The Story's Lesson.
Long-term success in a cutthroat real estate market requires a dedication to quality, an emphasis on fostering connections, and the ability to adjust to a constantly shifting environment rather than short cuts or fast fixes.

The experience of Team B shows that people who put community involvement, agent growth, and customer happiness first build a strong, long-lasting company. Building a seven-figure real estate team may not be easy, but if you have the long view, you can succeed in the cutthroat industry and leave a legacy of quality and client confidence.

In the realm of real estate, attaining sustained success is a significant obstacle, particularly when striving to establish a seven-figure team.

A strategic vision, resilience, and adaptability are required in the competitive market. Let's examine important factors to make sure your real estate team succeeds in the long run.

1.Client-Centric Approach:
Setting your clients' needs first is essential to developing a seven-figure real estate team. Understanding each client's specific demands and providing outstanding service are key components of a client-centric strategy. It's about developing relationships and trust, not simply about transactions. Contented

customers turn into your greatest
supporters.

2. Professional Development:

Provide for the advancement of your team's expertise. Maintaining current knowledge and developing one's skills is essential in the dynamic real estate market. Motivate your agents to seek out training and qualifications that correspond with current industry trends.

3. Adaptability:

This is crucial since market conditions are constantly changing. Seize the opportunity to quickly adopt innovative techniques and technology that can boost team productivity and improve the customer experience. It's critical to keep up with the latest developments in data analytics, virtual tours, and digital marketing.

4. Community Involvement:

Take an active part in your neighborhood. Establishing long-lasting connections and becoming a dependable resource in your community can result in recommendations. A positive reputation can be developed through organizing events, giving back to the community, and sharing market information.

5. Prioritize Quality Over Quantity:

It's simple to succumb to the lure of speedy transactions and instant rewards. On the other hand, putting quality above quantity frequently results in longer-term success. Customers value a comprehensive, customized strategy over a hurried, one-size-fits-all fix.

6. Building a Strong Brand:

Your brand is how your team is seen by your clients; it goes beyond a logo and tagline. Develop a brand that is synonymous with honesty, competence, and first-rate service. Brand consistency fosters trust.

7. Resilience:

Be prepared for obstacles and market downturns in the real estate sector. Variations in the economy and markets are unavoidable. For your team to succeed in the long run, they need to be resilient. When things are difficult, maintain composure and concentrate on your rehabilitation plans.

8.Market Analysis:

Examine market data on a regular basis to spot trends and business prospects.

Making educated selections is made possible by having a thorough understanding of both the local market's nuances and the larger economic environment.

9. Customer relationship management (CRM):

To handle client interactions and data, put in place an efficient CRM system. You may track customer preferences, nurture leads, and uphold enduring relationships with the aid of a well-organized CRM system.

10. Lead Generation Techniques:

Keeping a steady stream of new customers requires the development of efficient lead generation techniques. This entails realizing the potential of both offline and online strategies, including networking, social media, content marketing, SEO, and referrals.

11. Conversion Mastery:
Converting leads into clients is an ongoing process that calls for constant refinement. Your staff should be outstanding at recognizing each client's particular demands and negotiating on their behalf. Proficiency in the art of conversion guarantees a robust and devoted customer base.

12. Effective Systems:
Long-term success depends on effectiveness. Reduce operating expenses and increase productivity by putting in place efficient systems and processes. Tools and technology have a big role in improving operational effectiveness.

13. Financial Planning:

To guarantee the long-term financial stability of your team, prudent financial planning and budgeting are essential. This entails controlling spending, putting money aside for future opportunities for growth, and forecasting economic downturns.

14. Market Challenges:

Be proactive in your preparation for market challenges. Create plans to deal with downturns in the economy, changes in the competitive environment, and evolving consumer behavior. Challenges can be turned into opportunities for an agile team.

15. Keeping Ahead of the Competition:
Differentiation and innovation are your friends in a cutthroat market. Keep an eye

on your rivals, pinpoint any service gaps, and work to maintain your lead through better customer service.

The ultimate goal in building a seven-figure real estate team is to achieve long-term success. You may establish a long-lasting real estate company by putting these tactics into practice, staying client-focused, and being flexible in a cutthroat industry.

The Significance of Creativity and Flexibility
Innovation and Adaptability's Significance in Reaching Long-Term Success.

It is impossible to overestimate the importance of innovation and adaptation in the fast-paced real estate industry, where markets are continuously changing and competition is intense. These fundamental ideas must be embraced by real estate professionals if they are to create a seven-figure team and succeed over the long haul.

Innovation as a Growth Catalyst:
In the real estate sector, innovation is the key to sustained success. It entails being able to recognize and adjust to new trends, technology, and consumer preferences.

Here's how uniqueness can make your group stand out:

1.Technology Integration:
Use the newest real estate technologies to stay ahead of the curve. Advanced CRM systems, AI-driven market analysis, and virtual reality tours are just a few examples of the tools that may improve customer experiences, expedite workflows, and offer your team a competitive edge.

2. Excellence in Digital Marketing:
In the current digital era, having an online presence is essential. Invest in a thorough plan for digital marketing. To increase your reach and interact with potential customers, make interesting content, optimize your website for search engines, and make use of social media.

3. Environmental Sustainability:

Eco-friendly and sustainable techniques are becoming more and more prevalent in the real estate sector. Invent by adding eco-friendly designs, energy-saving techniques, and sustainable building materials to your listings.

4. Diverse Offerings:

Increase the variety of services you provide. Think about branching out into property management, commercial real estate, or real estate investing in addition to regular residential sales. These several sources of income can help you maintain long-term financial stability.

The Skill of Flexibility.

Being flexible is crucial in a real estate market that is highly competitive. Teams must adapt quickly to change in the market in order to remain relevant. This is when flexibility comes into play:

1.Recognize Trends and Shifts in the Market:

Consistently examine market data to spot changes and trends. For example, modifications to remote work schedules could result in fresh need for various kinds of attributes. Modify your strategy to take advantage of these changes.

2. Resilience to Economic Downturns:

Downturns in the economy are unavoidable. Establishing financial reserves and putting plans in place to withstand economic downturns will help your team get ready. Stabilizing your revenue might also come from providing a range of services, such as property management in hard times.

3. Adopting Agile Business Models: This is something you should think about. You can easily adjust to shifting client wants and market conditions with the help of these models. One example of flexibility during the pandemic was providing virtual property tours in response to social distance needs.

4. Customer-Centric Services: Never lose sight of your customers' requirements. Be prepared to modify your tactics in light of client preferences and feedback. Differentiating your offerings to fit specific client wants will make you stand out from rivals.

Establishing an Innovative and Adaptable Culture.

Long-term success in real estate requires your team to foster an innovative and flexible culture. In order to foster such a culture, follow these steps:

1.Ongoing Education:

Motivate your group to participate in continuing education. Give them access to workshops, certificates, and training so they can stay current with changes in the field.

2. Unstructured Communication:

Encourage unobstructed avenues of communication. During routine team meetings, encourage team members to discuss market shifts and contribute their creative ideas.

3. Testing and Experimentation:

Don't be afraid to try new things. Give your staff the freedom to experiment with new tactics and technology and evaluate their efficacy.

4. Modular Leadership:

Set a good example. As a leader, show flexibility in the way you make decisions. Your group will do the same.

In conclusion, creativity and flexibility are critical elements for thriving in a cutthroat real estate market and developing a seven-figure real estate team. Adapting to market changes, embracing new technologies, and cultivating an innovative culture will set up your team for long-term success in a field that is always changing.

Preserving a Robust Work-Life Balance

To achieve long-term success, a strong work-life balance is essential.

It's simple for professionals to become overwhelmed by the demands of their jobs in the fast-paced real estate industry. However, maintaining a solid work-life balance is essential to long-term success and thriving in a competitive market. Here are some reasons why finding this balance is crucial, as well as some tips for doing so:

Work-Life Balance's Significance:

1.Sustainability:

In the real estate sector, longevity is reliant on sustainability. A shortened career and burnout might result from trying to do too much at once. You will have the endurance for the long haul if you take a balanced approach.

2. Health and Well-Being:

Your physical and emotional health may suffer as a result of overworking yourself. Health problems might result from long-term stress, sleep deprivation, and disregarding one's own well-being. Living a balanced life lowers the chance of burnout and encourages good health.

3. Better Productivity:

Having a well-balanced life typically leads to better efficiency, despite the common misconception that more labor equals more productivity. You are better able to concentrate and make more thoughtful decisions when you are well-rested and stress-free.

4. Fulfillment:

Long-term success requires more than just monetary gain. You can find fulfillment in your hobbies, interactions with others, and other interests when your life is balanced, and this can improve your performance at work.

Techniques for Preserving Work-Life Harmony.

1.Establish Boundaries:

Clearly state what your personal and work hours are. Share these boundaries with team members, clients, and coworkers. Recognize your own boundaries and urge others to follow suit.

2. Arrange Tasks based on the Order of Priority:

Sort and arrange the tasks that are most important first. To free up time for what matters most, assign or contract out less important work. Purchase time management resources to aid in your organization.

3. Time management:
Develop your time management skills. To manage your time effectively, try the Pomodoro method, time blocking, and to-do lists. Minimize interruptions, particularly when working.

4. Self-Care Routine:
Make self-care a part of your weekly or daily schedule. Frequent physical activity, meditation, and engaging in hobbies can aid in stress reduction and relaxation.

5. Technology Utilization:
Make use of technology to make tasks go more smoothly. To handle client

interactions more effectively, automate repetitive tasks, hire virtual assistants, and spend money on customer relationship management (CRM) software.

6. Flexibility & Remote Work:

Welcome to work in a flexible environment. Include opportunities for remote work if at all practicable. Possessing the flexibility to work remotely or from home might improve work-life balance.

7. Delegate Duties According to Individual Abilities:

As your team in real estate expands, assign members of the team duties. Give them the freedom to manage chores and make choices to lighten your workload.

8. Regular Review:

Evaluate your work-life balance on a regular basis. Are you successfully managing your work and setting aside personal time on a regular basis? Adapt your plan as necessary.

9. Quality Over Quantity:

Put more of an emphasis on providing clients with high-quality service than on striving to serve a bigger clientele. Repeat business and increased referrals might result from high-quality work.

10. Learn to Say No:

When you're overburdened, it's important to gently turn down offers of assistance or duties. Overcommitting can throw off your work-life balance and cause stress.

Keep in mind that working smarter, not harder, is the key to long-term success in a cutthroat real estate market. A keystone of this strategy is sustaining a robust work-life balance. You can make sure that your career is long-lasting and fulfilling by putting your health first, using your time wisely, and striking a balance between your personal and work lives.

Leaving a Real Estate Legacy
Real Estate Legacy-Building.

It is a commendable objective for real estate agents to thrive in a competitive market and achieve long-term success. But it's also crucial to think about the legacy you create in the field. Making a long-lasting impression entails more than just making a profit; it also entails improving and advancing the real estate industry. Here are some tips for becoming successful in real estate and leaving a legacy:

1. Education and Mentorship:
Make an investment in the future of real estate professionals. Aspiring agents and team members will appreciate your knowledge and experience. By providing mentorship and educational opportunities, you enhance the general skill and professionalism of the sector.

2. Ethical Standards:
When it comes to your real estate dealings, uphold the highest ethical standards. Act with integrity, honesty, and transparency when conducting business. By acting morally all the time, you lead by example for other people in the field.

3. Community Participation:

Participate in the community by giving back to the areas you work in. Engage in neighborhood projects, fundraisers, and gatherings. In addition to helping those in need, supporting and improving the well-being of your community will improve your reputation as a socially conscious real estate agent.

4. Keep up with Technology:

Keep up with the latest developments in technology and industry trends through innovation and adaptation. Accept change and adjust to the evolving real estate market. The way the real estate industry is run may be significantly impacted by your capacity to make use of innovative technologies and tactics.

5. Thought Leadership:

Use thought leadership to impart your knowledge and skills. Compose articles, give speeches at business gatherings, or participate in debates concerning current issues and trends in real estate. Being a thought leader allows you to shape the industry's future.

6. Sustainability and Responsibility:

Integrate environmental responsibility and sustainability into your real estate operations. Promote eco-friendly building materials, energy-efficient dwellings, and conscientious land development. The environment and the real estate sector benefit from your efforts to be sustainable.

7. Professional Associations:

Participate in real estate associations for professionals. Participate in leadership roles, join committees, and influence these organizations' practices and policies. Industry norms can be influenced by active participation.

8. Networking and Cooperation:

Establish deep connections and cooperative efforts with colleagues in the field. Working together can result in creative fixes and industry breakthroughs.

9. Customer-Centric Approach:

Give top priority to client pleasure and outstanding customer service. You build a good reputation for yourself that reaches out to upcoming generations of real estate agents and buyers when you continually go above and beyond for your clients.

10. Continuous Learning:

Never stop learning with continuous learning. Keep abreast on the most recent rules, procedures, and trends in the industry. Maintaining your education level guarantees that you will always be a useful member of the real estate community. Making a meaningful and long-lasting impact on the real estate industry, your community, and the professionals that come after you is more important to leaving a legacy in the business than achieving financial success. You can support a flourishing and ethical real estate community for years to come by embracing mentorship, ethics, community involvement, innovation, and a dedication to positive change.

Conclusion

Conclusion: Building Your Legacy in Real Estate.

You've experienced the tactics, difficulties, and victories that come with learning how to create a seven-figure real estate team. Your adherence to this course demonstrates your commitment to building a successful future for your group as well as for yourself. Let's wrap up this book with a tale that perfectly captures what it takes to leave a lasting legacy in the real estate industry.

There once was an aspirational real estate agent named Sarah in a tiny town. She began her profession by tending to a tiny team, treating it like a fragile young tree.

With perseverance, commitment, and the knowledge imparted in these pages, her team developed into a profitable seven-figure enterprise. But Sarah knew her legacy extended beyond the balance sheet.

A young real estate agent called Sarah one lovely day when she was sitting in her office thinking back on her journey and asking for help. This agent had big goals but didn't know where to begin because she was fresh to the profession. After taking the phone, Sarah talked for an hour about her life experiences, observations, and life lessons.

Sarah understood the importance of what she had just done as she hung up. She was doing more than just developing a profitable company; she was leaving behind a legacy of wisdom, coaching, and direction for others. As her mentors had been for her, she had now turned into a source of inspiration.

Sarah's tale exemplifies the ultimate purpose of this book, which is to assist you in attaining financial success while creating a legacy that will motivate and uplift upcoming real estate generations. Getting to seven figures is not just about having money; it's also about making a difference in the lives of those in your community and among the professionals who look up to you.

As you wrap up the chapters in this book, keep in mind that creating a seven-figure real estate team is really a means to an end. It's about becoming financially independent so that you may support other people's success, develop moral behavior, and improve your community.

Your real estate legacy is determined not only by your financial success but also by the knowledge you impart, the moral principles you follow, the communities you touch, and the future generation of real estate agents you encourage. As you proceed, remember that the goal of your trip is to create a lasting legacy rather than just hitting seven figures.

Thus, accept your position as a leader, mentor, and source of inspiration for others. Keep coming up with new ideas and adjusting to the ever changing real estate market. Maintain the highest moral standards, cultivate an excellent culture, and make sustainability and accountability a constant priority in all that you do.

This brings our journey to an end. While creating a seven-figure real estate team presents many obstacles, there are also many chances to have a significant influence. We hope that this book's contents have not only increased your success but also stoked your desire to leave a lasting legacy in the real estate industry.

Recap of Key Takeaways

Recap of Key Takeaways:
In the book "How to Build a 7-Figure Real Estate Team," we have covered a wide range of crucial tactics, perspectives, and guidelines for creating a profitable and long-lasting real estate team. Here is a succinct summary of the most important lessons learned from this extensive guide:

1. Vision and Goal Setting:
Give your real estate team a clear vision
and establish short- and long-term
objectives. A clear course of action is
necessary for success.

2. Team Building:
Put together a group of gifted experts who
enhance each other's abilities and
qualities. Never forget that the most
precious asset you have is your staff.

3. Leadership:
Establish a favorable work atmosphere,
give direction, and lead by example to be a
powerful and successful leader.

4. Ethical Practices:
To gain the trust of your clients and your
team, always operate with the utmost
ethics.

5. Branding and Marketing:

To improve your team's exposure and standing in the industry, develop a distinctive brand identity and use successful marketing techniques.

6. Lead creation:

To maintain a constant stream of prospective customers, employ a range of lead creation techniques, both online and offline.

7. Conversion:

Learn how to turn leads into clients by getting to know them, going above and above with your service, and establishing enduring bonds.

8. Technology and Tools:
Use real estate software and technology to improve efficiency, simplify procedures, and give clients better service.

9. Financial Planning:
To guarantee the stability and expansion of your team's finances, create a solid financial plan and budget.

10. Scaling Your Business:
As your team expands, concentrate on hiring the best personnel, investing in training and development, and scaling your processes.

11. Adapting to Market Shifts:
Keep a step ahead of the competition, adjust to market shifts, and handle economic downturns skillfully to be ready for any market challenge.

12. Extended Success:
Innovating, upholding a solid work-life balance, and creating a lasting legacy in the real estate sector are all essential to long-term success.

These essential lessons offer a strong basis for developing a seven-figure real estate group. Keep in mind that being successful in the real estate sector involves more than just achieving financial goals; it also involves having a positive influence on your neighborhood, staff, and clients. In order to create a successful and long-lasting real estate team, keep learning, growing, and innovating.

Your Journey to a 7-Figure Real Estate Team

Sarah Mitchell, a newbie in the real estate industry, was apprehensive as she stood before Prestige Realty's stately entryway, which was one of the most prestigious agencies in the city, once upon a time in the busy metropolis of Metropolis.

Excitement and trepidation mixed together as she gripped her beautifully prepared resume. She was about to set out on a journey that would turn her into a seven-figure team leader in the real estate industry.
Sarah's tale started off in modest circumstances. Being raised by a single mother, she was instilled with the principles of perseverance and hard work at a young age.

She realized after getting her real estate license that she wanted to create her own real estate empire rather than merely work a job.

She began her career as a rookie agent with Prestige Realty. Her daily schedule consisted of long hours, door knocking, and endless phone calls. She encountered clients with a range of requirements and tastes, underwent rejection, and felt frustrated by the unpredictability of the market.

But Sarah was focused on being successful. She went to seminars, absorbed real estate books, and looked for guidance from the best in the business. She was aware that developing a seven-figure real estate team needed more than just property sales; it also required vision, leadership, and interpersonal skills. Sarah started assembling her crew as she developed her reputation and sharpened her abilities. She carefully chose people who shared her enthusiasm and vision for real estate. They set out on a mission to dominate the industry together.

There were difficulties along the way. There were ups and downs in the real estate market, and Sarah's team experienced some disappointments. However, she didn't waver, utilizing the newest technologies, learning how to convert people, and adjusting to changes in the industry.

Their diligence paid off. The team's name became a byword for reliability and quality over time. Sarah's clientele grew, and they began to recommend her. Her meticulous budgeting and financial planning guaranteed the team's growth and stability.

But for Sarah, being successful in the real estate market meant more than just making money. She recognized the value of taking care of herself and her loved ones, as well as striking a balance between work and life. She also made it a point to return the favor to the society that had helped to make her journey possible.

Sarah Mitchell has a seven-figure team and is not simply a successful real estate salesperson today—she's a real estate royalty. Her legacy goes beyond the homes she sells; her rise from inexperienced agent to successful businesswoman has motivated innumerable budding realtors.

In Metropolis, the name Sarah Mitchell is a byword for tenacity, foresight, and the steadfast conviction that anybody can make their real estate ambitions come true for seven figures with the correct team and diligence.

About The Book

Embark on a transformative journey in "How to Build a 7-Figure Real Estate Team," a comprehensive guide that unveils the secrets to success in the dynamic world of real estate. Written by seasoned industry expert Gary S. Nichols this book is your blueprint to creating a thriving real estate business that transcends financial milestones.

Inside its pages, you'll discover the strategies and principles that propelled Gary S. Nichols from a rookie agent to a real estate magnate with a 7-figure team. This book is not just about selling properties; it's a strategic roadmap for building an empire.

Learn how to navigate market challenges, adapt to shifts, and master the art of conversion. Discover the intricacies of assembling a dream team, defining goals, and fostering a culture that breeds success. From branding and marketing to leveraging technology and tools, Gary S. Nichols provides actionable insights and proven techniques that have stood the test of a competitive market.

But "How to Build a 7-Figure Real Estate Team" is more than a guide to financial success; it's a manual for achieving long-term prosperity. Dive into the chapters on work-life balance, maintaining a strong team culture, and leaving a lasting legacy. Gary S. Nichols shares the importance of innovation, adaptability, and strategic growth in sustaining a thriving real estate business.

Whether you're a seasoned professional or a budding entrepreneur, this book equips you with the tools to not only survive but thrive in the ever-evolving real estate landscape. Join the ranks of industry leaders who have turned their aspirations into reality, and let "How to Build a 7-Figure Real Estate Team" be your compass on the path to unparalleled success. Your journey to real estate royalty starts here.

About The Author

Meet Gary S. Nichols the mastermind behind "How to Build a 7-Figure Real Estate Team." With a wealth of experience spanning decades, Gary S. Nichols is a seasoned expert in the realms of real estate and investment. A visionary entrepreneur, Gary S. Nichols has not only weathered the ever-changing tides of the real estate market but has emerged as a triumphant leader, turning aspirations into a thriving reality.

Bringing a unique blend of strategic insight and practical wisdom, Gary S. Nichols has been a driving force in the industry, navigating through economic shifts, market challenges, and emerging trends with unparalleled acumen. Their journey from a budding investor to a stalwart figure with a 7-figure real estate team is chronicled in this groundbreaking book.

Beyond the pages of this guide, Gary S. Nichols is known for their commitment to excellence, innovation, and the art of building sustainable success. As a sought-after speaker and mentor, Gary S. Nichols has shared their expertise with countless professionals, empowering them to forge their paths to financial prosperity.

Get ready to embark on a transformative journey under the guidance of Gary S. Nichols. In "How to Build a 7-Figure Real Estate Team," they open the doors to their vast knowledge, offering readers a backstage pass to the strategies and principles that have defined their remarkable career. Whether you're a seasoned investor or a newcomer to the real estate arena, Gary S. Nichols is your trusted companion on the path to building a legacy of success in the world of real estate.